Praise for **THE ASSHOLE SURVIVAL GUIDE**

"First, the *No Asshole Rule* alerted us to the problem. Now, *The Asshole Survival Guide* offers the solution. This book is a contemporary classic — a shrewd and spirited guide to reducing our exposure and protecting ourselves from the jerks, bullies, tyrants, and trolls who seek to dispirit and demean. Now more than ever, with civility and decency under attack, we desperately need this antidote to the a-holes in our midst." — **Daniel H. Pink,** best-selling author of
To Sell Is Human and *Drive*

"This survival guide is here to help you from going insane. It's full of science-driven tips and strategies on how to deal with nasty bosses, manipulative colleagues, or other general jerks in your life."
— *W Magazine*

"Sutton offers a variety of techniques that people suffering the presence of difficult individuals at their work, in their sports teams, or just in everyday life can employ to deal with them or fight back. This is a small book but it could play a big part in making us treat others better." — *Forbes*

"If everyone had paid attention to the Stanford business professor's best-selling 2007 management manifesto, *The No Asshole Rule,* there would be no need for a follow-up. Yet here we are." — *Esquire*

"The crowded genre of workplace bullying books features clever titles . . . the best of the authors in the category is Stanford professor Robert Sutton, who published *The No Asshole Rule* a decade ago and returns now with a more fully developed plan of action."
— *National Book Review*

"Sutton's breezy writing style, combined with the wide array of anecdotes and stories from people who've written him about their difficulties, makes for an entertaining read . . . consider that the physical book itself might be a solution to an a-hole at work. Much like the effect Sutton's first book reportedly has had, simply leaving *The Asshole Survival Guide* prominently on your desk may send all the signal you need."

— *SmartUp*

"Bob Sutton is very wise and very funny, AND he can tell you exactly how to handle the unfortunate reality that into every life a few assholes must fall. *The Asshole Survival Guide* is destined to become your go-to resource whenever you find yourself dealing with people who would treat you poorly."   — **Susan Cain**, *New York Times* best-selling author of *Quiet*

"At last someone has provided clear steps for rejecting, deflecting, and deflating the jerks who blight our lives. Better still, that someone is the great Bob Sutton, which ensures that the information is useful, evidence-based, and fun to read."

— **Robert Cialdini**, author of *New York Times* bestsellers *Influence* and *Pre-Suasion*

"No matter what industry or profession you work in, you will always encounter people who are unpleasant, off-putting, or downright self-centered. Thank goodness Bob Sutton has provided us with such a well-crafted guide for surviving these jerks. It is mandatory reading for anyone who strives to endure, escape, fend off, and bring them down."

— **Chip Conley**, founder and past CEO of Joie de Vivre hotels, advisor and former Head of Global Hospitality and Strategy at Airbnb, author of four books, including the *New York Times* bestseller *Emotional Equations*

"With humor, understanding, and comprehensive research — and an ah-ha moment on every page — this is a must-have for leaders and climbing stars alike, from the expert on the subject. Bravo!"

— **Marshall Goldsmith**, author of the #1
New York Times bestseller *Triggers*

"This is the guide you need for handling the worst people in your life — and making sure they don't rub off on you. If you've ever had a horrible boss, client, or colleague, this book is bursting with advice that's often ingenious and always actionable. And if your world has been free of jerks, consider this an insurance policy."

— **Adam Grant**, *New York Times* best-selling
author of *Give and Take* and *Originals*,
and coauthor of *Option B*

"Assholes are like the weather — everybody complains about them but nobody ever does anything about them. Until, that is, Robert Sutton's *Asshole Survival Guide*. Sutton offers a wealth of helpful, and dare I say wise, suggestions about how to identify and deal with the assholes in your organization, or at least minimize the damage they do to the well-being and productivity of others. (I'd also suggest bringing it along to family reunions and PTA meetings.)"

— **Geoff Nunberg**, University of California
at Berkeley, author of *Ascent of the A-Word:
Assholism, the First Sixty Years*

"Reading *The Asshole Survival Guide* made me wistful. If only Bob Sutton's book had been available to help me deal with the full complement of first-class assholes I've encountered in my fifty-year professional life. No names shall be mentioned."

— **Tom Peters**, coauthor of the bestseller
In Search of Excellence

"As much as we try to avoid assholes, inevitably they appear in our lives. Bob Sutton gives us a menu of clear, thoughtful, and practical solutions for surviving and thriving in those painful situations. With cutting-edge research and real-life examples that are thought-provoking and often hilarious, *The Asshole Survival Guide* is an indispensable resource." — **Gretchen Rubin**, best-selling author of *The Happiness Project* and *Better Than Before*

"One of the biggest impediments to achieving a great workplace is assholes. Their behavior creates a hostile work environment that leads to decreased engagement, productivity, and employee loyalty. Bob Sutton has written a fantastic book that explains the severity of the problem and provides useful strategies for dealing with it."
— **Paul Purcell**, chairman and former long-serving CEO of Baird, ranked fourth on *Fortune*'s Top 100 Companies to Work For and renowned for its long-time "no assholes" policy

"It's hard to know how to react to a jerk, so *The Asshole Survival Guide* is a godsend. Obnoxious behavior is a double whammy. First, you feel mad at the other person. Next, you feel mad at yourself for your response/lack of response. It's being mad at yourself that is both hard to be aware of, and is most debilitating. With this brilliant and funny book, Bob Sutton saves you from fear, loathing, and self-loathing!" — **Kim Scott**, author of the *New York Times* bestseller, *Radical Candor*, cofounder of Candor, Inc., former executive at Google and Apple

THE ASSHOLE SURVIVAL GUIDE

HOW TO DEAL WITH PEOPLE WHO TREAT YOU LIKE DIRT

Robert I. Sutton

Mariner Books
Houghton Mifflin Harcourt
Boston   New York

First Mariner Books edition 2018
Copyright © 2017 by Robert I. Sutton

For information about permission to reproduce selections from
this book, write to trade.permissions@hmhco.com or to Permissions,
Houghton Mifflin Harcourt Publishing Company, 3 Park Avenue,
19th Floor, New York, New York 10016.

hmhco.com

Library of Congress Cataloging-in-Publication Data
Names: Sutton, Robert I., author.
Title: The asshole survival guide : how to deal with people who treat
you like dirt / Robert I. Sutton.
Description: Boston : Houghton Mifflin Harcourt, [2017] |
Includes bibliographical references and index.
Identifiers: LCCN 2017012053 (print) | LCCN 2017030882 (ebook) |
ISBN 9781328695925 (ebook) | ISBN 9781328695918 (hardcover) |
ISBN 9781328511669 (paperback)
Subjects: LCSH: Organizational behavior. | Interpersonal conflict. |
Bullying in the workplace. | Psychological abuse. | Interpersonal relations.
Classification: LCC HD58.7 (ebook) | LCC HD58.7 .S934 2017 (print) |
DDC 650.1/3 — dc23
LC record available at https://lccn.loc.gov/2017012053

Book design by Greta D. Sibley

Illustration on page 90 redrawn by Chloe Foster from a model
provided by the author.

Printed in the United States of America
DOC 10 9 8 7 6 5 4 3 2 1

To Eve, Claire, and Tyler.

Thanks for your laughter and love.

Contents

1 Eight Thousand Emails

I WROTE THIS BOOK to answer a question that I've been asked thousands of times. It takes different forms, but the essence is: "I am dealing with an asshole (or a bunch of them). Help me! What should I do?" Consider a few examples from my daily dose of asshole emails:

From a physician at a "deeply dysfunctional" hospital with "the most insensitive team chief imaginable":

What is an underling to do? I can put my head down, take care of my patients as best I can, and try to ignore the cruelty, but it is demoralizing to work in such an environment.

A Lutheran pastor in Illinois writes:

A great deal of the work in our church is done by non-paid individuals who, at times, hurt the feelings of fellow volunteers. Do you have any thoughts on what to do with mean people who volunteer their time?

A retired German manufacturing manager asks:

In my working life I have been fired at least three times through the doing of the Arseholes, "Sale cons," Arschlöcher, Stronzi and their like. What advice do I give my son so he doesn't suffer the same fate?

A Silicon Valley CEO writes:

With so many startups and so many Venture Capitalists who lack operational experience sitting on boards, I was wondering if you have done any work or thinking about boardholes (individual bad board members) or entirely dysfunctional boards which one might call "doucheboards."

And from a librarian in Washington, DC:

I am knee-deep in Russian assholes. Help!

Someone asks me a version of this question pretty much every day. It arrives in those emails and via Twitter, LinkedIn, and Facebook too. Students, colleagues, clients, friends, enemies, and relatives ask it at gatherings including classes, faculty meetings, weddings, and funerals. Strangers call my Stanford office about once a week to ask it. I've been asked for survival tips from cashiers at Costco and Walgreens, nurses and doctors at the Cleveland Clinic and Stanford Hospital, flight attendants from airlines including Air France and United, construction workers in San Francisco and Idaho, Uber drivers in Dubai and San Francisco, subway riders in New York City and BART riders in San Francisco, U.S. Marines in Afghanistan, a prison guard in Texas, several Catholic priests, a Jewish cantor (and a cantor's wife), fifty or so lawyers, and at least a dozen CEOs. In recent months, I've heard it from a surgeon in New York, the dean of students at a small liberal arts university, a U.S. Army psychologist, a group of undergraduates in a French university (via Skype), a Stanford police sergeant, my barber Woody, and even my mother. It's no mystery why they keep asking. It all started when I wrote *The No Asshole Rule* in 2007 (and a related essay for *Harvard Business Review* a few years before). I assumed that this asshole stuff would be a brief side trip and, within a year or so, I would return to my work on leadership, innovation, and organizational change. I was wrong. That little book touched a nerve. It took me a few years to accept that—no matter what else I write in my life or any other impact my other work has—I will always be known first and foremost as "The Asshole Guy." Some eight hundred thousand readers in the United States and dozens of other countries bought a copy of *The No Asshole Rule*—far more than my other books. The steady stream of emails, social media, traditional press inquiries, and disturbing, weird, or funny conversations about all things asshole have become parts of my life that I expect, (usually) enjoy, and try to handle with compassion and good cheer.

Many readers were drawn to *The No Asshole Rule* because they were besieged by jerks who left them feeling like dirt—and they sought relief. It does have a chapter on "When Assholes Reign: Tips for Surviving Nasty People and Workplaces." The main focus of that book, however, was on *building civilized workplaces*—not on dealing with assholes. *The Asshole Survival Guide* is devoted to strategies and tips that enable people to escape from, endure, battle, and force out bullies, backstabbers, and arses.

I developed these strategies and tips over the years. No matter what I was "supposed to" be working on during the past decade, I spent an hour or two most days thinking, reading, talking, and writing about assholes and their antidotes and—now and then—observing rude or abusive people in their natural habitats. The result is *The*

Asshole Survival Guide, which provides the best advice I can muster about how to deal with people who leave others feeling oppressed, demeaned, disrespected, or de-energized. I focus on the workplace. But the lessons here are pertinent to asshole problems faced by volunteers at nonprofits and schools; to jerks in churches, temples, and mosques; and to rude behavior in public places such as subways, airports, malls, and sports stadiums.

The strategies and tips here are shaped by scholarly research on demeaning and disrespectful people — which has grown like crazy in recent years. Google Scholar is a specialized search engine for scholarly books and articles; it's become the gold standard that academics use to find rigorous theory and research. A Google Scholar search on "abusive supervision" between 2008 and 2016 returns 4,910 scholarly articles and books. "Abusive customers" returns 282, "rudeness" 16,000, "incivility" 15,500, "bullying" 140,000, "workplace bullying" 11,800, "mobbing at work" 2,900, "road rage" 6,680, "air rage" 369, "phone rage" 92, "verbal aggression" 16,500, and "microaggression" 2,190. Yet my advice isn't meant to reflect an exhaustive and unbiased summary of scientific research on how to deal with jerks. These findings are instructive, but far from definitive and complete. Asshole survival remains more of a craft or skill than a science.

So lessons from these studies are blended with stories and solutions from less scholarly sources. *The Asshole Survival Guide* draws on assorted corners of the world and the World Wide Web — ranging from the *New York Times* to David Kendrick's superb post on online behavior, "What Makes a Fuckhead?" I also weave in lessons from my observations and original interviews — including work as a consultant and speaker at varied organizations (e.g., Amazon, Wal-Mart, Gallup, Google, luxury goods purveyor LVMH, KIPP schools, McKinsey, Microsoft, the Cleveland Clinic, Pixar, software firm SAP,

Twitter, and a Stanford program for National Football League executives) and fifty or so interviews (and less formal discussions) with people including social workers, baristas at Philz Coffee, nurses at the Stanford Hospital, Disney executives, human resources executives (notably Patty McCord, who was at Netflix for its first fourteen years), and researchers including Professor Katy DeCelles of the University of Toronto — who studies the causes of air rage, how prison guards deal with inmates, and the effects of temper tantrums by basketball coaches on players.

This book is also shaped by all those emails about assholes that people send me. I try to save each bit of correspondence in my rather disorganized system of three email folders ("NA Stories," "Bosses," "Asshole Survival Guide") and some sixty subfolders (e.g., "Asshole Bosses," "Asshole Underlings," "Brits," "Clients," "Asshole Companies," "Bystanders," "Public Life," "Sound Crazy," "Italian," "Online Assholes," "Fighting Back," "Got Out," "Wrong Way to Fight," "Success Stories"). I've kept about eight thousand such emails; most contain some variation of the question that this book tackles. Many of my correspondents also tell me about (successful and unsuccessful) survival methods that they've tried. And *The Asshole Survival Guide* also draws upon the 1,500 or so responses I wrote back to these emails, which include encouragement, advice, and follow-up questions.

THE DAMAGE DONE

In 2010, I talked with a young CEO who worried he wasn't enough like the late Steve Jobs — that his career and his little start-up would suffer because he was calm and he treated people with respect. I've had a lot of conversations like this over the years. As I did with this CEO, I always point to pundits and researchers who argue that *Assholes Finish First* — that's what (now-retired) "professional asshole" Tucker Max titled his book for "dudes and bros." Or, in recent years, I point to articles such as Jerry Useem's 2015 *Atlantic* piece on "Why It Pays to Be a Jerk."

My Stanford colleague Jeff Pfeffer argues that treating people like dirt can be a path to personal success because, as he explained it to Jerry Useem, when you put a python and chicken in a cage together, the "python eats the chicken." I agree that there are circumstances where leaving others feeling oppressed, demeaned, disrespected, or de-energized can help adept jerks vanquish competitors and attract allies (who kiss up, in part, because they hope to be spared the asshole's wrath, backstabbing, or dirty looks). Treating others like dirt and being selfish can also help people triumph in pure "I win, you lose" situations — where there is no incentive to cooperate with others now or in the future. And chapter 6 of this book considers when and why giving assholes a taste of their own medicine is an effective way to fight back (I do warn, however, as my wife Marina puts it, "When you throw shit at other people, it often gets all over you too").

That said, my reading of that big pile of research indicates that pundits and professors who celebrate bullies, takers, and narcissists are exaggerating the spoils and downplaying the harm that assholes inflict on themselves (especially in the long run). This conclusion dovetails with numerous other academics, including Wharton's Adam Grant (he studies the fate of "givers" versus "takers"), the University of Southern California's Christine Porath (she studies incivility), and the University of California's Dacher Keltner (he studies emotion and power dynamics). As work by these professors and many other researchers would predict, there is a long list of winners who have succeeded *without* treating people like dirt: this includes Apple CEO Tim Cook, Netflix CEO Reed Hastings, Berkshire Hathaway CEO and investment icon Warren Buffett, the late comedian and actor Robin Williams, celebrity chef Anthony Bourdain, television producer Jenji Kohan (creator of *Orange Is the New Black*), and executive producer and writer Shonda Rhimes (of *Grey's Anatomy* and *Scandal* fame) — the list goes on and on. And, in 2015, I talked again with that CEO who fretted back in 2010 because he wasn't loud, overbearing, and selfish enough. I can't tell you his name, but he still isn't an asshole, and his company now has more than a thousand employees, and he is a billionaire.

I also had a revealing conversation with Pixar's founder and president Ed Catmull (who worked closely with Steve Jobs for twenty-five years) about the widespread belief that Jobs succeeded, in part, because he was overbearing, temperamental, and insensitive — the myth that enticed that young CEO to wonder if he ought to behave the same way. Catmull agreed that Jobs had a well-earned reputation "for poor behavior early in his career." Catmull emphasized, however, that many writers, biographers, and filmmakers miss a crucial part of the story: that Jobs changed for the better after he was "kicked out" of Apple and suffered a slew of setbacks at his high-end computer company NeXT and at Pixar in the early years. As Catmull put it, Jobs "wandered in the wilderness" for a decade. Catmull explained that "in the course of working through and understanding these failures, and then succeeding at Pixar, Jobs changed; he became more empathetic, a better listener, a better leader, a better partner." Catmull said that the "more thoughtful and caring" Steve Jobs was the one "who created the incredibly successful Apple." Jobs remained a tough negotiator, a challenging person to argue with, and a perfectionist; but Catmull observed that Jobs's greatest successes came only after he abandoned the notorious mistreatment of others that plagued his early years.

Yet, even if the asshole lovers are right, and being all asshole all (or most) of the time is a path to personal success, treating others like dirt does so much damage that *even if you are a winner and an asshole, you are still a loser as a human being in my book.*

I am not just saying this because I am The Asshole Guy. Although evidence about how to best deal with assholes is murky and incomplete, the negative impact of demeaning and disrespectful people on their victims is crystal clear. Thousands of studies in diverse disciplines confirm how high the total cost of assholes (TCA) is to groups, organizations, and society — and especially to targeted individuals. Consider just a taste of this damning pile of data.

Hundreds of experiments show that encounters with rude, insulting, and demeaning people undermine others' performance — including their decision-making skills, productivity, creativity, and willingness to work a little harder and stay a little later to finish projects and to help coworkers who need their advice, skills, or emotional support. For example, an experiment with doctors and nurses in Israeli neonatal intensive care units entailed creating encounters with a rude American health-care expert. This ugly American insulted the skills and intelligence of the Israeli doctors and nurses; he told them that he was "not impressed with the quality of medicine in Israel" and said the medical staff that he observed in Israel "wouldn't last a week" in his American department. The belittled doctors and nurses performed far worse (compared to a control group) on tasks including diagnosing a medical mannequin's physical deterioration, perforated bowel, and cardiac problems.

In other words, that American asshole rattled the Israeli health-care professionals so much that it undermined their ability to treat sick babies. Rude patients have similar effects on physicians; research conducted in the Netherlands suggests that doctors make more errors when they diagnose demanding and aggressive patients who question their competence compared to when they diagnose more civilized patients.

In 2011, renowned science fiction writer William Gibson retweeted a thought by "Notorious d.e.b." (@debihope on Twitter) that went viral: "Before you diagnose yourself with depression or low self esteem, first make sure you are not, in fact, just surrounded by assholes." Much evidence supports @debihope's advice. Studies of rudeness and incivility — on air rage by loud, obnoxious, and insulting airplane passengers, phone rage, road rage, and "pedestrian aggressiveness syndrome" — show that such nastiness is contagious and can undermine a victim's mental and physical health for days or weeks. Thousands of studies of bullied children show that the psychological damage includes weaker academic performance, along with mental and physical health problems. And children who were bullied by peers may be haunted the rest of their lives — they are prone to adult problems including higher arrest rates, financial struggles, depression, and heavy smoking.

Research on workplace assholes (where this book focuses) reveals that demeaning and disrespectful peers, underlings, customers and clients, and, especially, bosses (or "bossholes") can damage performance and well-being. To illustrate, assembly-line workers react to verbal abuse with emotional detachment and lower productivity. New nurses bullied by veteran nurses and doctors put forth less effort and develop less empathy for patients. Service employees who are subjected to customer aggression (e.g., rude gestures, yelling, swearing, glaring) report more mental and physical health problems and are less committed to their jobs. Similarly, service employees who observe customers abusing their colleagues (rather than experiencing it firsthand) suffer a similar fate.

And treating others like dirt is contagious — so if you work with a jerk (or, worse, a bunch of them), you are likely to become one too. A 2012 study documented how such shit rolled downhill: abusive senior leaders were prone to selecting or breeding abusive team leaders, who in turn, ignited destructive conflict in their teams, which stifled team members' creativity.

The list of damages done by workplace assholes goes on and on: reduced trust, motivation, innovation, and less willingness to make suggestions; increased waste, theft, absenteeism, and surliness. Professor Bennett Tepper of Ohio State University and his colleagues estimated that abusive supervision costs U.S. corporations $23.8 billion a year (based on absenteeism, health-care costs, and lost productivity). That was in 2006; the estimate would be far higher now. Workplace jerks also wreck their target's physical and mental health — triggering anxiety, depression, sleep problems, high blood pressure, and poor relationships with their families and partners. Long-term studies in Europe show that working for a bosshole increases the risk of heart disease and premature death. For example, a twenty-year study that tracked six thousand British civil servants found that when their bosses criticized them unfairly, didn't listen to their problems, and rarely praised them, employees suffered more angina, heart attacks, and deaths from heart disease.

You get the idea. It doesn't matter whether the assholes around you are getting ahead or (more likely) screwing up their lives, careers, and companies. They pose a danger to you and others. I wrote this book to help you protect and defend yourself and the friends, colleagues, customers, teams, and organizations that you hold dear from these mean-spirited people and their vile words and deeds.

WHAT'S AHEAD

The next six chapters consider how to assess, escape, endure, fight, and force out bullies, backstabbers, and arses. Chapter 2 on "Asshole Assessment: How Bad Is the Problem?" provides six diagnostic questions to help you to assess how dangerous, difficult to deal with, and damaging a given asshole problem is—if it requires minimal, modest, or major protective measures. The next four chapters consider the pros, cons, and nuances of different survival strategies: Chapter 3 shows how and when to "Make a Clean Getaway." Chapter 4 provides "Asshole Avoidance Techniques," methods for reducing your exposure to assholes that you can't escape from—at least for now. Chapter 5 is about "Mind Tricks That Protect Your Soul," or ways of thinking about and reacting to assholes that reduce the damage to you and others. Chapter 6 digs into tactics for "Fighting Back." It spells out effective and sometimes mischievous means for reforming, repelling, and removing assholes—and for bringing jerks down a notch or rendering them powerless paper tigers.

This book ends with chapter 7 on "Be Part of the Solution, Not the Problem." I show what it means to embrace the no asshole rule as a personal philosophy, a theme that runs through and glues this book together. The rule isn't just for teams and organizations. It is a personal commitment that shapes how you judge people, the kind of individuals you hang out with and work with, and your determination to detect, dampen, and defeat disrespectful actions made by yourself and others.

A BIAS-BUSTING MANTRA

Be slow to label others as assholes, be quick to label yourself as one.

Keeping this mantra in mind primes you to avoid falling prey to your knee-jerk reactions — to slow, stop, and reverse the initial judgments that you make about suspected jerks. It prepares you to get more from this book. Saying it and living it can help you — and those you support, teach, or coach — do a better job of understanding when bullies and backstabbers are (and are not) rearing their ugly heads, why they are doing their dirty work, and how to deal with them. It's among the most crucial lessons that I've learned over the years about how to think about and deal with possible assholes.

Bending your judgments in this direction counteracts biases that are baked into us human beings — even the most wonderful, caring, and unselfish of us. As you will see in chapter 7, research by psychologists shows that we are often clueless about or downplay our weaknesses and mistakes, develop inflated opinions of our skills and abilities (especially in areas where we are least competent), and are prone to blame others for our problems (even when it's our own damn fault). This research suggests that if you act like an asshole, or protect or enable others' demeaning and disrespectful behavior, you aren't likely to admit these unflattering facts to yourself or anyone else. So it is no surprise that national surveys by the Workplace Bullying Institute between 2007 and 2014 found that over 50% of Americans report they've experienced or witnessed ongoing episodes of bullying — but less than 1% admit to subjecting others to such repeated mistreatment. One reason for this big gap is that some people are mighty thin-skinned and even downright paranoid — so they overreact to repeated small or imagined slights and attribute evil intent to people who don't intend to hurt them (and who may even be trying to help them). The main reason, however, is that people who act like assholes are often blind to their bad behavior and how others experience it.

This mantra isn't a cure-all for limited self-awareness. But it is a counterforce to the automatic and often flawed interpretations that we are all prone to make. Being slow to label others as assholes gives you time to consider other explanations and develop empathy for the alleged assholes — rather than reacting with instant and sometimes unnecessary hurt and anger. Being quick to label yourself as a jerk, or at least pausing to consider that you could be part of the problem, can counteract the oh-so-human predilection to deny and downplay our imperfections and sins. And this mantra helps you avoid fueling vicious circles where you and your alleged tormentor both feel wronged, and perhaps yell at each other, *"I am not the asshole, you are."*

2 Asshole Assessment

HOW BAD IS THE PROBLEM?

ASSHOLES USE A HOST OF DIRTY TRICKS to torment their targets. Consider these terrible tidbits from my emails: Ear flicking. Shouting. Smiling warmly as she whispers in his ear, "You are a loser. I am going to bring you down." A "passhole" (passive-aggressive asshole) who treats people as if they are invisible and ignores their requests. Inviting only her "favorites" to the office holiday party. Interrupting him "five times in five minutes." Asking him, "Are you done with that piece of shit yet?" Holding mandatory Sunday staff meetings. Taunting her for working too hard. Glaring, name-calling, wearing a "shitty morning face," constant teasing, and treating everything as an emergency and making every molehill into a mountain.

Fawns over and flatters colleagues to their faces, then spreads vicious lies behind their backs. Writes an employee up for arriving to work fifteen minutes EARLY. Flies into a rage over a late water delivery for the office cooler. Gives her one compliment in eight years. Uses the F-word in almost every sentence. Breathes like Darth Vader when she gets mad. Fires employees over the phone, insists other colleagues do it too. Tells a coworker that customers feel sorry for her because she has "sad eyes." Calls a customer "an ugly bitch" who dresses in "rags" behind her back. Tosses a lit cigarette at him. Grabs her and bites her on the arm "leaving a bruise."

Alas, these examples probably don't shock you given the remarkable range of rude and demeaning acts in traditional and social media stories these days. Yet some of this madness would still seem fake or wildly exaggerated without photographic evidence. For example, a 2016 video of Shanxi Changzhi Zhangze Agricultural and Commercial Bank in China posted online by Channel NewsAsia shows a manager who — in front of hundreds of colleagues — humiliates eight workers by hitting each four times on the buttocks with a large stick because "they didn't work hard enough." One of the employees spanked as part of this "performance breakthrough course" cried, stumbled, and appeared to be in considerable pain. Or check out @passengershame on Twitter, where people post real pictures and videos of airplane passengers doing appalling things such as putting their dirty bare feet on the ceiling and on fellow passenger's armrests. One video shows a woman popping the zits and pulling out the nose hairs of the man sitting next to her; in another a woman ignores and then insults a flight attendant who asks her to extinguish a cigarette.

Researchers have labeled and sorted hundreds of different bad behaviors. Carleton University's Kathryne Dupré and her colleagues measured "customer-initiated workplace aggression" by asking 428 workers if, and how often, they had experienced, seen, or heard about eleven despicable customer behaviors. These include "said something to spite you," "glared or gave dirty looks to you," and "targeted a false accusation at you." Bennett Tepper from Ohio State University developed the Abusive Supervision Scale, which asks fifteen questions about how often "my boss" does things like "puts me down in front of others," "makes negative comments about me to others," and "invades my privacy." Yale University's Philip Smith and his colleagues studied "The Rude Stranger in Everyday Life." They list twenty-one kinds of rudeness (e.g., "Pushed in front of me" and "Took up too much personal space"), which occurred in twenty-seven locations (e.g., "In a supermarket," "On a freeway/highway," or "At an airline terminal").

In other words, these stories and studies identify so many different kinds of assholes, who operate in such varied places, and do their dirty work in so many ways, that no one-size-fits-all survival strategy will work for every jerk. If anybody tells you that they have a step-by-step, complete, and surefire cure for all your asshole problems, they are lying to themselves and to you. I can't promise easy or instant relief. *The Asshole Survival Guide* can, however, help you decide which survival tricks and moves are best for navigating the particular ugliness that you face, figure out ways to suffer less harm, and — sometimes — triumph in the end. The chapters that follow provide practical tactics and tips to consider using as you develop and update your own custom survival strategy.

The first step is to figure out how dire things are for you or for those you hope to help. Beware of first impressions. Snap judgments are dangerous. Nobel Prize winner Daniel Kahneman recommends that anybody in a "cognitive minefield" — that is, who faces a confusing, difficult, and distressing challenge — ought to first slow down, study the situation, consider different paths, and talk to some smart people before settling on a plan and taking action. The dangers of snap judgments and virtues of slowing down to think are well documented. Dr. Jerome Groopman urges fellow physicians to resist their penchant for making instant diagnoses of patients (most doctors take less than twenty seconds). Groopman's mentor taught him that often the best advice is "Don't just do something, stand there."

It's better than making a quick and bad diagnosis and inflicting the wrong treatment on a patient. This chapter helps you avoid making snap judgments about problems with possible assholes. It poses six diagnostic questions to think about and discuss with people you trust. The first question helps you determine if you've got an asshole problem at all. If yes, the next five questions help you figure out how bad it is — and thus how diligently (or desperately) you need to work on it. The worse that things are, the harder you ought to work at crafting and carrying out a survival strategy. It becomes more crucial to put other demands aside and to focus on coping with and taming your tormentors. And chances are higher that you will encounter more surprises and setbacks along the way — requiring even more trial and error and shifts in strategy.

HAVE YOU GOT A PROBLEM?

As we've seen, endless antics are attributed to assholes. Certainly some despicable actions — physical assault or sexual harassment, for example — provide unassailable evidence that the asshole label is warranted. Yet there are vast differences in cultural, industry, and organizational beliefs about when and why people deserve the label. There are also big variations in how different personalities react to the same potentially repugnant actions and people. Moves that leave one person feeling offended or oppressed may not bother or even register with another, might amuse another, or might be taken as approval and even affection by yet another. For example, a former U.S. National Football League player pointed out to me that, after a great play in a game, slapping a teammate on the head or butt and calling him "one bad motherfucker" is high praise on the field—but that kind of aggressive behavior can get you fired or arrested elsewhere.

The first diagnostic question follows from the late writer Maya Angelou's assertion that "at the end of the day people won't remember what you said or did, they will remember how you made them feel." Certainly, many victims can never forget what abusive people have said and did to them. But Angelou's words ring true to me. The people who provoke me to think "what an asshole"—the ones who stick in my craw and drive me crazy—are those who trigger painful feelings in me or in those I care about. The same goes for people who tell me their asshole stories: they are tormented in wildly varied ways but are similar in that somebody is doing something that leaves them feeling pissed off, put upon, discouraged, or otherwise emotionally unsettled or hurt.

My focus on the targets' feelings also means that such "victims" aren't automatically absolved of all blame. This contrasts with the usual asshole naming and shaming game. Whether it is academics who measure bullying, abuse, or aggression with questionnaires, or people who post disturbing images on @passengershame, the assumption is often that these vile acts are committed by evil and guilty perpetrators and then reported by innocent victims or bystanders. But if you want to *really* understand an asshole problem and how to best tackle it, consider how *your* quirks, background, and biases shape your feelings. Taking responsibility for your feelings—and understanding what drives those of other targets or witnesses—helps you (or them) figure out how to limit the damage. It also helps to come to grips with how you (or they) might be making it all worse—for example, by being too thin-skinned, or placing excessive or irrational blame on the alleged jerks, or behaving like an asshole too.

So here's the first diagnostic question. Ask yourself or those people who you are trying to help:

1. Do you feel as if the alleged asshole is treating you (and perhaps others) like dirt? Do encounters with an alleged asshole (or a pack of them) leave you feeling oppressed, demeaned, disrespected, or de-energized — or all of the above?

If the answer to this question is a solid "no," then there isn't a problem, or at least not one that requires much attention. But if the answer is "yes," that means that you or others are suffering psychological harm and it would be wise to take protective measures. Just bear in mind that not all asshole problems are created equal. Some are worse than others.

HOW BAD IS IT?

A marketing manager wrote me about the "A$$hole Factory" where he worked for years. He said it was so broken that "someone should tent the building and spray it with A$$hole insecticide." The "Factory" had "blistering A$$hole family members running the show" who routinely yelled at employees and each other, who "scowled and growled," and who, the manager said, "spoke to me like I was a five-year-old child."

He listed a litany of offensive and bizarre moves by the ruling family, such as, "If I was eating something, a bag of potato chips for example, the president would walk into my cubicle, stick his hands in the bag, then look at me and say, 'Can I have some?'" The blight spread to this manager's immediate boss as well, who started out as "optimistic, friendly, driven, and trustworthy," but soon turned cruel and two-faced. The manager confessed that he turned into an "Asshole" too. As he told it, "I was losing my temper with vendors on the phone; my stress level was getting too high to manage; and I started to send more scathing emails. It also started to affect my personal life, as I would come home from work and lose my temper with my partner for no reason." After seven years, he finally got out, but not before suffering much damage and inflicting much of the same on others.

This case both horrifies and fascinates me because it took so long for the manager to realize how corrosive the "Factory" was to him, his coworkers, his partner, and even the vendor he flamed with rude emails. He didn't come to grips with how terrible it all was until *after* he escaped. A quick glance at the accompanying list of diagnostic questions suggests how bad this situation was: he felt as if he was treated like dirt, it lasted for years, the same people were abusive to him again and again (they were "certified assholes"), it was a systemic disease, he had less power than most of the jerks, and he suffered mightily.

Alas, we humans have a remarkable capacity for denial and delusion. That is, if he had realized how bad things were, I believe that manager would have taken more rapid and effective steps — in particular, escaped years earlier. Regardless of whether you are facing a horrible predicament like him — or subtle and less clear-cut problems — it helps to just stop, think, and dissect the situation. Ask yourself the five remaining questions — and recruit people who you trust to get their perspective and advice too.

HOW BAD IS IT?

Six Diagnostic Questions

1. **Do you feel as if the alleged asshole is treating you (and perhaps others) like dirt?** During or after interactions with the alleged asshole or assholes, do you feel oppressed, demeaned, disrespected, or de-energized? If so, you better start crafting a survival plan.

2. **How long will the ugliness persist?** If it is just a short episode, then you might be able to put it past you fairly quickly. But if it goes on day after day, or was a brief episode that keeps haunting you and others, then you need to devote greater attention to developing and using protective measures.

3. **Are you dealing with a temporary or certified asshole?** If you are dealing with a temporary asshole, you might just let it pass, and wait until he or she starts acting like a civilized human being again before giving some negative feedback, or perhaps just try a gentle intervention on the spot. But if you and others are besieged by someone who is all asshole all the time, then you need to act with more care and forethought, as you've got a more dangerous and damaging problem on your hands.

4. **Is it an individual or a systemic disease?** If you are dealing with one or perhaps two assholes in what is otherwise a sea of civility, then — while you are still at risk — you are most likely surrounded with people who can help and support you. The main risk is that nastiness can spread quickly like a contagious disease. But if you are living in

Jerk City, and every day feels like a trip down Asshole Avenue, you not only are taking flak from every direction and likely suffering much harm; you also have fewer potential allies.

5. **How much more power do you have over the asshole?** If you have far more power than the asshole does, then you have a broader set of options — it's easier to leave or get rid of that jerk, for example. But beware of overconfidence; just because you are the top dog or rich and famous doesn't mean you can do what you want — or that you have as much power as you imagine. If you have less power, and that bully can hurt you, you are at greater risk. You've got to think more deeply about your strategy, and then devote extra effort to recruiting allies around you who can protect you.

6. **How much are you really suffering?** This is the bottom line. What drives one person crazy may not bother another at all. You may be especially thin-skinned. But if you are dealing with people who leave you feeling deeply oppressed, demeaned, disrespected, or de-energized, then you've got to start doing something now — and something that is fairly time-consuming and drastic — in order to survive.

2. How long will the ugliness persist?   Even a brief insult, slight, or sign of disrespect can have lasting effects. The studies of rude strangers by Yale sociologist Philip Smith and his colleagues found that even episodes that last a few seconds — such as being bumped into by someone at the shopping mall or encountering a driver who steals your parking space and then flips you off—have effects on targets that can linger for weeks or even months. These range from being more tolerant and polite to "becoming more hardened to other people in general." You might dismiss people who stay pissed off, upset, or otherwise affected by a brief incident as just being a bunch of thin-skinned wimps who just need to get over it. But such lingering effects make more sense when you consider the most disconcerting episodes.

On July 12, 2016, for example, CNN news anchor Don Lemon talked on the air about a racist comment that an acquaintance had made at a restaurant. Lemon and another African American were part of a group (the rest were Caucasian) that was having an animated conversation about a murderous rampage by a sniper in Dallas that happened a few days before. The attack left five police officers dead and seven wounded—the victims were Caucasian and the sniper was African American. Lemon said that one of the white people asked the other African American at the table, "How does that make you feel, as a nigger?" Others in the group immediately responded to the N-word with angry accusations and demands for an apology; Lemon said nothing but experienced a blend of outrage and curiosity that surprised him.

Although it was days after the incident, Lemon looked discouraged during his on-air reflection and said the incident still troubled him—that it forced him to realize how deep racial bias still runs and how naïve it is to pretend that racism doesn't exist even among seemingly enlightened and educated people.

Certainly, being exposed to racist comments and insults day after day is worse than a single incident. And if the marketing manager at that "A$$hole Factory" had quit after a month—rather than seven years—he would have been damaged a lot less. But the lesson from that racist incident reported by Don Lemon — or other brief but jarring incidents — is that the duration of the ugliness ought to include the length and depth of the aftershocks. If people keep talking about it, arguing over it, or fretting about it, or it otherwise still haunts them, then the emotional damage isn't really over. Yet, on average, research on everything from abusive supervision to bullied schoolchildren shows that the longer and more frequently that a target is treated like dirt, the greater and more long-lasting the damage will be.

3. *Are you dealing with a temporary or certified asshole?* All of us are capable of being temporary assholes under the wrong conditions. There are endless reasons that, now and then, we might treat others like dirt — being tired or in a rush, feeling powerful, or having an overwhelming desire to bring down some high-and-mighty jerk are among the many triggers. As I wrote in *The No Asshole Rule,* "It is far harder to qualify as a certified asshole: a person needs to display a persistent pattern, to have a history of episodes that end with one 'target' after another feeling belittled, put down, humiliated, disrespected, oppressed, de-energized, and generally worse about themselves."

If you are dealing with just a temporary asshole, someone who usually treats others with warmth and respect, you probably don't need to take much — if any — action. It's often best to just say nothing or to just leave the scene. Or, if it is someone you know and normally like, you might treat their hostility as a sign they are simply having a tough day and need emotional support.

We all have bad moments. Years ago, I was having lunch with Bob Gibbons, an economist from Massachusetts Institute of Technology. I am a psychologist, and I confess, there is much about the field of economics I don't like (for example, numerous studies show that the more exposure that students have to economics, the more selfish and greedy they become). In any event, when I sat down next to Bob that day, I was in a foul mood and took it out on him. I said something about how most economists are selfish assholes. That certainly wasn't fair to Bob; he had done nothing to provoke my harsh comment, and he is one of the kindest, most giving, and understanding academics I know from any field of study. But rather than getting angry, Bob gave me a gentle smile and asked me if I had a tough night with Eve, our infant daughter. Bob was right. I was grouchy from a sleepless night with a sick kid. I apologized and stopped insulting Bob.

I was a temporary asshole that day.

But here's something curious. Sometimes, being a temporary asshole can improve a subordinate's performance. That is, when typically civilized and socially adept people spew unexpected venom, they might do so for strategic reasons. Targets may interpret a rare flash of anger or outburst from their boss as negative feedback that they deserve. And it may fire them up to try harder. So, especially in competitive situations, temporary assholes who berate, glare at, or ignore people whom they usually treat with warmth and respect just might bolster performance.

Consider an intriguing study. Researchers Barry Staw, Katy DeCelles, and Peter Degoey found evidence for such strategic nastiness in a study of 305 halftime locker room speeches by the coaches of 23 high school and college basketball teams. The speeches were recorded, which enabled these researchers to link how angry each halftime speech was (the degree of "unpleasantness") to changes in team performance in the second half of the game. They found that, up to a point, coaches who expressed negative emotion *did* spark improved performance. But coaches who were flaming assholes, who had the most extreme outbursts (e.g., intense anger, raging verbal abuse, throwing things), *drove down* performance.

The differences between temporary and certified assholes were especially instructive. Coaches who were usually pleasant sparked bigger performance boosts from their (occasional) outbursts compared to those coaches who were consistently unpleasant. So being all asshole all the time as a coach didn't work (especially being a flaming one). But an occasional strategic outburst seems to be effective because "targets" construe their temporary tormentor as trying to motivate them to try harder and to be smarter — they don't dismiss it as just the usual ranting from a certified asshole who berates them constantly.

As with all judgments about assholes, you will make better decisions about how bad things are and what to do if you are slow to conclude that a person — or a group of people — deserves to be anointed as "certified." For example, people who enforce high standards, demand respect from others, and aren't especially warm and likable — but do not undermine, demean, or ignore others — may upset those they hold accountable and be unjustly labeled assholes (at least behind their backs). But when tough people are also persistently and unnecessarily rude, disrespectful, and insulting, they deserve to be deemed certified assholes.

Captain Holly Graf of the U.S. Navy, for example, was proud to uphold "very high standards" for her crew. And to "let them know when they are not meeting them." In March of 2010, the *Telegraph* reported that, because of her "toughness," "brilliant seamanship" in her prior commands, and fierce determination, Graf became "the first American woman to take charge of a US Navy cruiser." But it all began to unravel for her when a top-level investigation — prompted by multiple complaints by her direct reports — led the Navy to relieve Captain Graf of her command of the 9,600-ton USS *Cowpens*.

According to the *Telegraph*, "One of the worst incidents came as the *Winston S Churchill* left a Sicilian port under Capt Graf's command on the eve of the Iraq War . . . As she entered choppier waters, a shudder ran through her hull. Capt Graf wrongly thought it had run aground, and her response was not the epitome of cool-headed leadership that is so admired among sailors. She grabbed the Royal Navy officer, who later told investigators that Capt Graf had 'got in my face and screamed "F****** *****. You ran my f****** ship aground."'"

The U.S. Navy's investigation found that Graf displayed "cruelty and maltreatment" to subordinates over a seven-year period, which earned her the nicknames that sailors called her behind her back, including "the Sea Witch" and "Horrible Holly." Of thirty-six witnesses interviewed, twenty-nine provided firsthand accounts of incidents where Graf had "demeaned, humiliated, publicly belittled and verbally assaulted" subordinates. The investigators found that Captain Graf repeatedly called her senior officers "idiots" and told one, "Take your God-damned attitude and shove it up your ass and leave it there." Graf was, it seems, a clueless asshole. She was "incredulous at the accusations" and told investigators that "her words were not meant to be taken personally."

Unfortunately, Captain Graf created fear and mistrust in her followers, rather than stoking the courage, skill, and confidence she intended. This troubling story also demonstrates that when certified assholes mistake unnecessary cruelty for necessary toughness, they can suffer self-inflicted damage when their many sins come to light.

4. Is it an individual or a systemic disease?   A professor from Europe told me, "My university is like an airport for assholes, one lands here every few minutes." He said a big part of the problem was that rude, arrogant, and selfish faculty members were more likely to be offered and accept jobs at his university than civilized professors. Assholes tend to breed like rabbits because of what psychologists call similarity-attraction effects. As Robert Cialdini documents in his classic book *Influence: The Psychology of Persuasion*, there is far more evidence that "birds of a feather flock together" than "opposites attract." That beleaguered European professor also described — much like that marketing manager who worked at the Asshole Factory for seven years — how even when civilized faculty were hired, they soon started acting like the rest of the jerks.

Such "infection" problems happen because emotions are remarkably contagious — bad moods, insults, rudeness, and sabotage spread like wildfire. For example, Emily Hunter from Baylor University and Lisa Penney from the University of Texas studied responses to difficult customers (who are rude, are loud, make excessive demands, and so on) among 438 food service employees (servers, hosts, bartenders, cashiers, and managers). The food service workers admitted to reciprocating the rudeness in a host of ways. Making fun of customers behind their backs, lying to them, making them wait longer, ignoring them, and arguing back at them were among the most common means of payback. In addition, servers confessed to even more extreme "negative behaviors" including refusing a reasonable request, insulting a customer, increasing a tip without the customer's permission, and contaminating food — which is why the researchers titled their article "The Waiter Spit in My Soup!"

When places are plagued with hostility and disrespect, there is nowhere to hide. There is malice toward many, and it can be conveyed in multiple directions. Either people don't realize they are turning mean just like everybody else or they become strategic assholes — returning fire to defend themselves from the creeps that surround them. And because the exposure is relentless, and often more intense, systemic asshole problems are more dangerous and difficult to cope with than isolated pockets of nastiness — or a single jerk — in a sea of civility.

Be careful, however, not to mistake one or two bad experiences or unpleasant people for a rotten system. This mistake is easy to make when the culprit pretends that treating you like dirt is a corporate policy — but he or she is really just a renegade asshole. Barry Staw — one of the researchers who studied the outbursts by basketball coaches — observes that individual jerks sometimes justify their mistreatment of others by "dressing up" like organizations. Consider the surly airline employee or local bean counter who denies your requests and claims it is "company policy" or who keeps you waiting for hours or weeks and tells you to quit complaining because they are just following "standard operating procedures" that are applied to everybody. The truth is, they are really just jerks pretending to be organizations.

Or, it might be the person who sits next to you every day, like the California sales rep who wrote me about a peer who claimed that he monitored exactly what time she and others arrived at work each morning because he was acting on behalf of senior management. He often berated and even cussed colleagues out for being just a minute or two late. It took the sales rep a while to figure out that management didn't want him or anyone else to be so picky or disrespectful. She finally confronted this jerk, asking, "Since when are you the self-appointed hall monitor/time clock here?"

He was "truly shocked" and stammered out that he was just assisting coworkers as a "mentor." The sales rep said, "I immediately replied and got very close to him, looking straight into his eyes, 'Well it is more like *torr-mentor*. So knock it off.'" As this sales representative discovered, when individuals dress up as organizations, sometimes they twist, exaggerate, or even defy the letter or spirit of the real rules, and will try to belittle, dismiss, frustrate, or ignore you, because they are insecure, lazy, on a power trip, or plagued by other personal quirks. But once you out them, their house of cards just might collapse.

Finally, be wary of how rapidly a single asshole, or just a few of them, can ruin a once civilized team or organization—especially if bullies and backstabbers take charge or move into other powerful roles. As I discuss next, the more powerful that these assholes are (especially compared to those who they target and torment), the more dangerous and difficult they are to deal with.

5. How much more power do you have over the asshole?   When a bully operates alone, has no allies, and has little power compared to you or anyone else, they aren't likely to pose a big threat. That's what happened once the sales rep exposed her *"torr-mentor."* Or consider the fate of another powerless jerk.

Last year, I went to a baseball game at the beautiful San Francisco Giants' home stadium. Toward the end of the game, some choice front row seats below me became vacant—the occupants had left, at least for a while. A fan from a less desirable section moved to those seats with his wife and baby daughter. A Giants' "Guest Services" employee noticed and came over and asked them to move back to their original seats, explaining that they hadn't paid for the preferred seats, the occupants might be back, and there was a park policy against moving from less expensive to more expensive sections of the stadium (that is consistently enforced). The Giants' employee was a friendly older gentleman and I had noticed the regulars in that section — season ticket holders — often bantered with him during the game.

Unfortunately, the father reacted to this employee's request with a stream of insults and expletives; his wife's face turned bright red and she left with their daughter immediately. The father spent another five minutes or so ranting at and insulting the Giants' employee; then he finally accepted defeat and left. As he walked up the stairs toward where I was sitting, several fans hollered "jerk" and "asshole" at him. They were disgusted with him for berating a well-liked employee who was just doing his job and ruining the sweet mood on that lovely afternoon. I watched him — perhaps too intently — as he passed my seat. He caught my eye and hollered, "I am not the asshole here, am I?" I didn't answer. There was no point because he was so powerless and he knew it. Everyone was against him: the Giants' organization, the other fans, even his wife.

Then there are people with modest but real power — and who take sick satisfaction from frustrating and pushing others around. In *The Fire from Within,* for example, author and anthropologist Carlos Castaneda expressed disdain for "minor petty tyrants" — people with limited power who are determined to "persecute and inflict misery." Petty tyrants wield power over some narrow but unavoidable domain and lord it over victims in small-minded, uncaring, and demeaning ways. The "Rule Nazi" is a common and especially vexing breed. As Columbia University's Heidi Grant Halvorson wrote on the *Harvard Business Review*'s website in 2016: "They cling to the rules like Leonardo DiCaprio clung to that door in *Titanic* — as if their lives depend on it. And they make sure everyone else does too, even when the rule doesn't make sense or stands in the way of productivity."

I think of that bank clerk who insisted that I complete a long form all over again because I made one small mistake — rather than allowing me to simply correct it and initial it. Or the administrators at Stanford who wrote, and enforced, their rigid rules with such gusto that I was required to write a personal check to Stanford for $14.12 after spending too much money on wine at a recruiting dinner for a faculty candidate (four people attended and we each had a single glass of the cheapest wine on the menu). As another, more flexible, administrator pointed out to me, it probably cost Stanford $25 to process my check.

A hallmark of petty tyrants — including many Rule Nazis — is that their power over a narrow domain is coupled with low prestige; they simmer and sulk about the lack of respect they get. This mix of power and low social status creates a deadly brew — it provokes them to take out their frustration and resentment on others. Nathanael Fast of the University of Southern California and his colleagues did an experiment that triggered this brand of abuse by university students. The researchers labeled some students "Workers," told them that their role would entail menial tasks, and that fellow students "tend to look down on the Worker role and don't have admiration or respect for it."

Other students were anointed "Idea Producers" and told they would be performing important tasks and that fellow students looked up to and respected the position. Students in both groups were then asked to dictate which "hoops" their partner (who was imaginary, but they believed was real) would have to jump through to qualify for a $50 drawing. The "hoops" ranged from activities that weren't demeaning at all (e.g., "tell the experimenter a funny joke") to creepy and humiliating (e.g., "say 'I am filthy' five times" and "bark like a dog three times").

The results? The lowly "Workers" took out their resentment on their imaginary partners by selecting far more demeaning acts for them to perform. In short, petty tyrants are rarely in a position to ruin your life, but often wield their limited authority to make you suffer (and to make themselves feel more important).

And just because you are the boss doesn't mean that you have more power than your underlings. A veteran Silicon Valley CEO related a lesson that he learned (the hard way) about the dangers of two-faced and socially adept underlings. This CEO does everything possible to hire and encourage "blunt, no BS" employees who confront him with facts and strong opinions about problems, don't hesitate to critique his conclusions, and tell him when he has been too hard (or too easy) on people. The CEO emphasized that, so long as employees aren't selfish or crazy, he doesn't mind when such conversations get heated. He believes that problems are much easier to tackle when the facts and associated feelings are put on the table — so long as there is mutual respect and (when necessary) heartfelt apologies after people cool down. To him, the most dangerous employees are "grinfuckers" who smile, flatter him, and nod in agreement with him — but then stab him and the company in the back.

Two-faced grinfuckers have certain signature moves. They pretend to enthusiastically agree with every decision you make or idea that you have, but rather than telling you when they disagree, they never actually implement the ideas, or do the exact opposite, or intentionally implement the decisions or ideas so badly that failure is inevitable. Then they bad-mouth you and other colleagues behind your backs for your terrible ideas and judgment.

6. *How much are you really suffering?*   No matter how you answered the other "Asshole Assessment" questions, this is the bottom

line. It isn't much fun to be annoyed or upset by demeaning customers, colleagues, bosses, volunteers, coaches, teachers, students, or strangers. But if the toll they take on you or others is *generally mild,* while you might want to start taking some relatively simple and easy protective measures, there is probably no immediate need for all-consuming, urgent, or extreme moves. On the other hand, if you or other people are getting sick, experiencing deep malaise, doing crummy work, or running for the exits, it's time for more urgent and extreme measures.

Remember, it can take only one horrible person to justify a full-blown asshole emergency, like the supervisor who wrote me that she was plagued with constant headaches, stomach problems, and insomnia by the onslaught of insults and political backstabbing from her departmental secretary. On the other hand, you just might be somebody who isn't bothered all that much by spending your days knee-deep in jerks — perhaps because you are thick-skinned or because the prize at the end is so important that you refuse to let them get to you.

I suspect both of these defenses worked to protect my friend Becky Margiotta when she was a "plebe" or "fourth-class cadet" at the United States Military Academy at West Point some twenty years ago. For their entire first year at the academy, plebes are required to "ping" at all times: march at a brisk 180 steps per minute, greet all superiors, perform an exhaustive list of menial tasks to total perfection, clean their rooms to white-glove standards, take a twenty-credit-hour course load, and participate in mandatory athletics, all while maintaining their military bearing and showing no emotion at all times — regardless of how much they are screamed at, insulted, or humiliated by upper-class cadets. When plebes make real or imagined mistakes (which happens constantly), it is not unusual for one or more upper-class cadets to berate them mercilessly.

If you assess Becky's predicament as a plebe with the prior "Asshole Assessment" questions, it seems pretty bleak. The hazing went on for Becky's entire first year. Those upper-class cadets heaped the abuse on her day after day, it was systemic, and she had no power. Yet, rather than letting those antics bruise her soul, Becky focused on how creative and amusing her tormentors were. As I discuss in more detail in chapter 5 on "Mind Tricks That Protect Your Soul," this kind of mental "reframing" helped Becky survive and thrive that first year at West Point. She went on to a successful military career, which included serving as a Special Operations officer.

BE CONFIDENT, BUT NOT REALLY SURE

I've urged you to resist making snap judgments about assholes and I have warned you about the dangers of overconfidence. That CEO who despised "grinfuckers" used one of the best antidotes to such delusions. He sought out and surrounded himself with people that he trusted to tell him the truth (rather than what he hoped to hear) about the severity and nuances of challenges that he and the company faced — and when he was screwing up. To borrow a lesson from Wharton professor Adam Grant's best-selling book *Give and Take*, it is smart to treat every asshole survival problem as a two-way street — where you both offer and ask for help. By giving help to troubled targets and witnesses as they try to size up and deal with jerks, you not only do good deeds; you equip yourself to withstand and to battle the malice and incivility in your own life. Your allies will usually feel obliged to return the favor, to help support, protect, and fight for you. And you will learn secondhand lessons that can help you to deal with your own asshole problems down the line. It's more efficient — and less painful — if you don't make every mistake yourself, no matter how instructive each might be. As a saying sometimes attributed to Eleanor Roosevelt goes, "Learn from the mistakes of others. You can't live long enough to make them all yourself."

Finally, the best way to strike the right balance between reckless action and paralyzing doubt is captured in rock star Tom Petty's line in "Saving Grace": "You're confident but not really sure." As I wrote on the *Harvard Business Review* website in 2010, that's what wisdom means to organizational psychologist (and my intellectual hero) Karl Weick. Wise people "have the courage to act on their beliefs and convictions at the same time that they have the humility to realize that they might be wrong, and must be prepared to change their beliefs and actions when better information comes along."

So take a little time to figure out how bad your predicament is and what you ought to do about it. Then charge forward with fierce resolve. But stay on the lookout for clues about little things that aren't working — and that your entire strategy is wrong and needs to be massively revised or junked. That's the kind of wisdom that Tom Petty and Karl Weick are talking about.

3   Make a Clean Getaway

I BELIEVE in quitting.

Legendary American football coach Vince Lombardi was wrong when he said, "Winners never quit and quitters never win."

Consider the case of convenience store cashier Misty Shelsky. She quit after William Ernst, owner of the Iowa-based QC Mart chain, "offered a $10 cash prize to workers who could predict which of them would next be fired." Shelsky and several other employees resigned when they realized that the company memo about the contest wasn't a joke. As she told the *Des Moines Register* in October 2011, "It was very degrading. We looked at that, then looked at each other, and said 'OK, we're done.'" Other QC Mart employees stayed but wrote management to express strong objections. When Shelsky applied for unemployment benefits, owner Ernst challenged the claim because she had resigned and not been fired. Judge Susan Ackerman awarded Shelsky benefits because Ernst had "created a hostile work environment" and called the competition "egregious and deplorable."

Getting out can provide sweet relief from a certified jerk or from a place where jerks rule the roost. Leaving the scene can also save you from brief but dreadful encounters. Numerous studies show that people who face, or simply witness, mean-spirited acts often react by leaving and avoiding the scene of the crime thereafter. The research by Yale sociologist Philip Smith and his colleagues on rude strangers found that over 50% of the 585 victims that they interviewed reacted with some form of "exit" — leaving or looking away in response to being pushed or bumped, hollered at, spat at, tailgated, and other indignities.

Dana Yagil of the University of Haifa shows that "when the customer is wrong" and treats service employees like dirt, they react by taking sick days and then resigning because they fear more abuse in the future. Vile bosses and coworkers drive employees and customers out as well. Bennett Tepper's study tracked 712 employees in a medium-sized midwestern city: those with abusive supervisors were more likely to voluntarily quit their jobs. And Christine Porath of Georgetown University and her colleagues found that when customers witness employees who are "uncivil" to each other, they become angry at the establishment, bad-mouth it, and take their business elsewhere.

Yet there is just a TENDENCY for people to flee from jerks. Many people can't or won't escape. Some are just stuck. Once the door of that train, airplane, or bus closes, if you can't change seats, you are condemned to deal with the nearby jerks for the duration of your trip. Or you might be stuck in a bad job or workplace: employees in Tepper's study who were trapped — who didn't leave abusive bosses because it was hard to find other work — were less satisfied with their jobs and more depressed; they also suffered elevated emotional exhaustion and conflict between work and family.

People who can bail out, but don't, often stick around for good reasons. Perhaps the harm isn't bad enough to make other options less attractive. Some people suffer mightily but believe what they are doing is so crucial and satisfying in other ways that they tough it out. Others feel obliged to stick around and protect the bullies' most vulnerable targets; they become, in effect, "human shields" who pride themselves in taking the heat for weaker victims. And some stay because they are determined to battle and defeat their tormentors.

People who can't or won't get out can especially benefit from the tactics for reducing exposure in chapter 4, the mind tricks for protecting your soul in chapter 5, and the means for fighting back in chapter 6. Unfortunately, too many people with serious asshole troubles who can and ought to escape engage in self-deception. They delude themselves into believing that things aren't really so bad or they are trapped when they really aren't — and thus doom themselves, and those they drag down with them, into taking far more unnecessary crap for far longer than necessary.

ASSHOLE BLINDNESS

The marketing manager in chapter 2 who endured seven years at the "A$$hole Factory" told a story that is all too common. It took him far too long to realize how much he was suffering, that he had better options, and to just flat-out quit.

I've heard hundreds of similar reports. An IT services employee wrote me about the "clenched anger, cold asshole" that he struggled to please and protect himself from for eight years. His ordeal adds a troubling twist: if you wait too long, the exit options that you once had may evaporate. His boss never insulted employees or had outbursts; rather, he said, "What she had was a hard, cold rage and the iciest eyes I have ever dealt with." This bosshole was highly suspicious and always interpreted errors or mistakes as being intentional, had no empathy at either "the practical or emotional level," never admitted she was wrong even once during those eight years, and created a Catch-22 where if he took initiative on a project, she reacted with "irritated criticism"; when he didn't take initiative, she lambasted him for inaction. He finally gave up and quit in 2015. By then, this poor fellow was having trouble getting a new job because he couldn't get good references, which he could have received the first couple years on the job. He regrets not leaving earlier, wonders if he should have gone over her head to complain, and feels shame for putting up "with her crap so long."

Neither he nor anyone else ought to be ashamed of putting up with this unnecessary abuse — that should be reserved for the perpetrators. Yet this story is instructive. He was afflicted with what I call "Asshole Blindness," where people don't realize or underestimate how dire an asshole problem is, how much they and perhaps others are suffering, and how important it is to get out as soon as possible.

Asshole Blindness is fueled by the one-two punch of *habituation* and *deluded justifications.* A bully, blowhard, or coldhearted creep — or a pack of them — can be like a terrible smell. At first the stink may disturb and disgust you. After a while, however, you get used to it and don't notice or dwell on it as much (if at all). That's habituation and it seemed to afflict the manager at the A$$hole Factory described in chapter 2; everyone was so mean, he was so unpleasant, and there was so much unhappiness around him for so long that the hideous scene became something that seemed normal and he didn't think about it much after a while.

Yet, especially when asshole problems are severe, and jerks keep doing their dirty work in varied ways, it's tough to tune them out completely. So people deceive themselves (and sometimes others) with half-truths and lies that prevent them from accepting just how bad things are, how long it has lasted and will go on, or how much damage is being done. A big reason that people develop such delusions stems from what academics call "escalating commitment to a failing course of action" or "the sunk cost fallacy." In other words, you know things suck, but you have already put so much time and effort into it that, as I explained in *The No Asshole Rule*, you are afflicted with too-much-invested-to-quit syndrome. This syndrome fuels twisted perceptions and self-destructive behavior because "we justify all the time, effort, suffering, and years and years that we devote to something by telling ourselves and others that there must be something worthwhile and important about it or we never would have so much of our lives sunk into it."

Think of the manager at the A$$hole Factory and the IT employee who served the "clenched anger, cold asshole." Every additional week, month, and year created greater pressure on them to justify why they had voluntarily continued to stay in such a bad situation, which led them to stay on and on — and to conjure up more and more reasons why they ought to keep suffering rather than to cut their losses and quit their lousy jobs. Beware, however, that such escalation dynamics can take hold very quickly — experiments by psychologists and economists show that if you make a public commitment to something, and work hard on it for just a few minutes, abandoning a decision, belief, or group becomes difficult.

Check out my list of justifications that fuel Asshole Blindness, the "Ten Lies That People Tell Themselves." These are common rationalizations that people use to explain why they haven't made a clean getaway. Sometimes they are wise and true. Yet, too often, they are bullshit, half-truths and lies that people tell themselves. Like the insurance company clerk who wrote me: "For six years I was abused and I should have done what you say and got out as soon as I could. But you get comfortable and used to the abuse. You even think you are successfully managing the abuser's behavior with your behavior.

Ridiculous I know. I suffered everything you mentioned including depression, anxiety and just plain unhappiness."

Are you living in a fool's paradise like that clerk? Or do some of these "Ten Lies" below describe how people around you are trying to justify their failure to leave a bad situation (or to even consider the possibility)?

ASSHOLE BLINDNESS:
Ten Lies That People Tell Themselves

1. **Denial about the present: "It's really not that bad."** It actually is a terrible situation — you are living in a fool's paradise.
2. **Imaginary improvement: "It's really getting better."** This is wishful thinking; things are as bad as, or worse than, ever.
3. **False hope: "Things are going to get much better soon."** You keep hoping — after all, you are an optimist. But the brighter tomorrow that you keep wishing and hoping for hasn't happened. And there is no good reason to believe it ever will.
4. **Tomorrow never comes: "I will leave for something better right after I finish this one important thing."** Then there will be one more thing, then another, then another. Life is messy. If you are waiting to tie a neat and pretty bow on it, and to leave at the perfect moment, you may wait forever.
5. **It hurts so good: "I am learning so much and making such great connections that the abuse is worthwhile."**

But is all the damage you and those around you are suffering really worth it? And aren't you worried about turning into an asshole too (or perhaps it is too late)?

6. **The savior complex: "Only I can make things better. No one else can replace me."** So if that's true, why are things so bad in the first place? Is it possible that not only are you suffering, but you are powerless to fix things? Or that you are unwittingly fueling the asshole problem and someone else would be better equipped to deal with it?

7. **I am not a wimp: "Sure, it's bad. But I am tough. It's not affecting me."** Hmm. I wonder if the people around you would agree.

8. **I can turn it on and off: "Sure, it's bad. But I am adept at 'compartmentalizing' so it doesn't really affect my friends or family."** What do friends and family say behind your back?

9. **Self-righteous suffering: "Sure, it is bad for me, but it is so much worse for others, I have no right complain."** Anything could always be worse. Martyrdom is a lousy excuse for staying in a terrible situation.

10. **The grass will be even browner: "It's bad here, but it would be even worse for me elsewhere."** Sure, no place is perfect. And some places might be worse. But have you really checked out your other options? This smells like a lame excuse.

Consider one more cautionary tale. A police officer from the Midwest wrote me how he put up with humiliation and ostracism at the same department where he had once enjoyed respect and success. In his early years, he rose from a patrol officer, to sergeant, to lieutenant, to acting chief and had always received glowing performance evaluations. Then a new city manager came in and, within six months, had demoted him back down to sergeant and then to patrol officer. The city manager explained to the officer that he was demoted, and others promoted, because, as he said, "Yes, you can do the job, but I want someone who is an asshole." The officer had other options but elected to endure these demotions and indignities including "social isolation" and the "silent treatment" for years. He left the department only when, after taking a military leave to serve in Afghanistan for a year (he was a member of the National Guard and called up for active duty), the city slashed his pay by almost 50% and stripped him of all his seniority. Then he quit and hired a lawyer.

Alas, this officer knew how bad his situation had become years before he left for Afghanistan — and he also had opportunities to join other police departments. But he fell prey to at least two of the delusions on my list. He told himself things weren't that bad and kept expecting things to get better — although he was under siege and things actually kept getting worse. The officer was also proud of the thick skin he developed during his over twenty years in the U.S. Marines and National Guard — an admirable quality in a soldier or police officer, but it proved to be a double-edged sword, as the "I am not a wimp" factor provided further justification for staying put.

A SMART GETAWAY

The "take this job and shove it" story about JetBlue flight attendant Steven Slater is classic. Slater had good reason to be pissed off at a passenger and fed up with his job. The *Guardian* reported that, before their plane took off from Pittsburgh on August 9, 2010, Slater had "been drawn into a fight between two female passengers over space in the overhead bins." In the process, he was accidentally hit hard on his head by their luggage. When the flight landed in New York "one of the women, who had been forced to check in her bag rather than carry it as hand luggage, was angry that it was not immediately available." She swore at and insulted him.

Slater was so fed up that he got on the microphone and cussed out passengers, grabbed two beers, and then activated and slid down the emergency escape slide. Slater's brazen getaway made him a folk hero. He was celebrated on talk shows and attracted more than twenty thousand Facebook fans. Yet in the end, as the *Guardian* reported, he lost his job, did $25,000 of damage to the plane, and caused flight delays. Slater was convicted of criminal mischief, given a year of probation, and required to pay JetBlue $10,000 in restitution. Slater expressed regret and said he "cracked under pressure because of his terminally ill mother, recently deceased father and health problems of his own, including HIV."

YOUR OPTIONS AND APPETITE FOR RISK

Yes, you should try to get away from assholes, but don't be an idiot about it. Alas, in retrospect, Steven Slater's fifteen minutes of fame probably wasn't worth it for him. Fantasies about dramatic exits or exacting revenge are good fun — but acting on them may hurt you more than your tormentors. And resisting the temptation can be tough. When people feel as if they are being treated like dirt, many feel a mighty strong urge to resign in abrupt or confrontational ways.

That's what studies by Anthony Klotz and Mark Bolino suggest; they conducted the most extensive research I've found on different "resignation styles." Professors Klotz and Bolino found that "bridge burning" and "impulsive quitting" occurred in about 15% of resignations (about 70% of resignations happened in less dramatic or in more civilized ways). But employees who felt they had been treated unfairly, had an abusive boss, or disliked the people they worked with were especially prone to use these angry and instant resignation styles. And, as you might expect, bridge burning and impulsive quitting triggered negative reactions in their supervisors.

The upshot is that if you are angry at your wicked organization, boss, and coworkers, you are probably tempted to make a fast and fiery exit. *But do so only with extreme caution:* such impulses can be dangerous because, if you act on them, it just might provoke some powerful and mean-spirited people to make you pay for it later. That's why, when people threaten to quit abruptly, do it in reckless ways that burn bridges, or both (even if it isn't in as dramatic a fashion as Steven Slater did), the first question I ask is "What are your other options?" The second question is "How much risk are you willing to take?"

To illustrate, a young attorney who was a year into a two-year clerkship for a U.S. federal judge described to me why, after talking to her mentors from law school, she decided to endure a second year in a corrosive workplace. Federal clerkships are prestigious positions for young attorneys — they involve doing everything from "ghostwriting opinions to fetching coffee and faxes for your judge." She had a similar position the year before with a wonderful judge and fellow clerks, but in her new job, "I entered onto the scene with two co-clerks who yell and belittle each other (and me) at every chance." The judge set the tone by throwing one tantrum after another; he flew into a rage over silly things such as "a late or incorrect water jug delivery." She added, "My co-clerks are probably depressed; it's understandable. One of them gets very angry and bangs his phone on his desk violently when he's upset."

Yet this lawyer decided that bailing out on the clerkship was even worse than staying: she had "massive" student debt to pay off and quitting was "career suicide"; future employers would see her as damaged goods. My immediate, knee-jerk reaction when she decided to stay in that cesspool — where she worked twelve hours a day, including most weekends — was she should quit, perhaps even pull a Steven Slater. But when I considered her debt and the career-limiting effects of resigning, I had to respect and support her decision to stay. She just didn't have better options. At least she knew that with every passing day, she was getting closer to the end of her two-year "sentence." In contrast, quitting makes more sense if you have good exit options, an appetite for risk, or both. A different attorney wrote that she finally escaped a "terrible job that was sucking my soul and making me miserable" and that she had started her own solo law practice and was happier than she'd ever been. And, although I urge people to beware of the risks of burning bridges as they say good-bye, I was amused that she placed her resignation letter in a copy of *The No Asshole Rule* and gave it to her oppressive and soulless boss.

Finally, as the study of outbursts by basketball coaches in chapter 2 suggests, if you are known as a hothead, then leaving in a huff probably won't surprise or concern anyone. But if you are seen as being even-tempered and upbeat, and leave with a fiery attack, your unexpected explosion may be taken as a sign that the problem is THEM and not YOU. So you might even bring down the local assholes with you. Keep in mind that this "Kamikaze Method" is risky.

If you use it, you better have other options lined up and be prepared for bad-mouthing and backstabbing by your former associates.

But sometimes it works, as it did for an even-tempered engineer who finally "snapped." He wrote me about his "I quit and I'm taking you down with me" method. Before this engineer exploded with rage at his boss, he had carefully documented her relentless abuse (but not yet shared it with management). Then, in a heated meeting, he explained to top management exactly why he was quitting; he "let them know they are culpable for all the mental anguish and turnover and poor results stemming from the asshole." This outburst had the intended effect: "Two hours later she was walked out. Now the department is doing great and actually producing instead of trying to manage the reactions of a lunatic."

CAN YOU JUST MOVE?

A Stanford graduate student told me that his wife and kids resisted going to church on Sundays because they dreaded encounters with a family of braggarts and bullies so much. Then his family switched to an earlier service that the despised family never attended: the student's wife and kids not only stopped resisting and complaining about going to church; everyone came back from church in far better moods. The Lord works in mysterious ways.

To stick with places of worship, the wife of a Jewish cantor in New York City wrote me that her husband had worked for a horrible rabbi. But the husband figured out how to switch to a synagogue with a wonderful rabbi that he knew across town — and how much happier and healthier he was, she was, and their children were all as a result.

Research on managers and leaders shows why — rather than leaving a current employer — finding a new job, boss, team, or department in the same organization might be the best strategy. Decades of research by Gallup, and more recent research by the "People Analytics" group at Google too, confirm the old saying "people leave bosses, not companies." Whether you work for a company like Google that routinely tops *Fortune*'s "100 Best Companies to Work For" list or at companies like Express Scripts, Sears, or Xerox that the career website Glassdoor rated as among the ten worst places in 2016, there are still big differences between the worst and best bosses and teams in your organization. And, as an insider, you probably have more precise information about where the toxic versus terrific people reside.

That's why smart organizations like Salesforce.com make it easy for employees to switch internal teams. When my Stanford colleague Huggy Rao interviewed Salesforce executives Chris Fry and Steve Green in 2012, they explained that teams were encouraged to actively recruit engineers from within the company, and that engineers who elected to leave an old team for a new one did not need permission from their old bosses. Chris and Steve told us that, each year, about 20% of engineers decide to switch to another team — and when a boss keeps losing members and can't recruit new ones, senior management takes that as a sign that the leader isn't treating people right, isn't competent, or both. Chris and Steve have since left Salesforce, but when we checked with current executives in late 2016, they reported the same policies remain in place and this "internal labor market" among Salesforce's four-hundred-plus engineering teams continues to help them keep people who would otherwise leave the company.

In other organizations, people transfer to different locations or jobs where fewer irate and inconsiderate customers will plague them.

Consider a study of stress among French bus drivers led by researcher Nathalie Louit-Martinod. Her team found that drivers struggled to cope with packed buses, streets crowded with rude drivers and pedestrians, and obnoxious passengers who insulted, sexually harassed, and spat at them. Drivers were also harangued for being late, driving too fast, and driving too slow. The stress caused some drivers to just quit. But many stayed, in part because seniority gave them the opportunity for some relief, for example, by transferring to less crowded routes and to areas where passengers were known to be more civilized. And one company operated both buses and trams: most bus drivers transferred to a tram as soon as possible because it had a separate cab in the front, which reduced contact with passengers and was seen as more prestigious and dignified work.

BRIEF BUT DREADFUL ENCOUNTERS

When you face short run-ins with people who are rude, demeaning, and disrespectful, and who really get under your skin and annoy you, sometimes it's just better to get away from them for a while.

A product manager wrote that when he was stuck in meetings with colleagues or clients who drove him crazy, and he started worrying he would do or say something he would later regret, he just stood up and said, "Forgive me, but I need to call my eighty-five-year-old mother." It was such a good and wholesome reason that no one ever objected — and his mother was always delighted to hear from him. Or you might ask yourself, if the movie, play, party — or even the wedding — that you're attending is going to continue for a while, if you feel under siege, surrounded by overbearing or argumentative people, if you can leave at the first less-than-rude opportunity, you should.

In school, we are all taught to stay in our seats until we are dismissed, which enables teachers to maintain discipline and create a more orderly classroom. But these lessons in conformity can hurt us later in life. Much as you look for the fire exits in a theater or hotel, it is wise to always keep looking for socially acceptable exit options. For example, after using Lyft and Uber to get around San Francisco for several years, I've learned that — while most drivers are wonderful — every now and then I get one who rants on about politics, asks me offensive personal questions, or — recently — pressed me to buy an electronics device that he sold on the side. So long as we are in a safe place, and in a locale where other drivers are plentiful, I ask to be let out early and then summon a new car. It adds a few minutes to my journey and costs me a few bucks, but I always feel so much better.

TROLLS AND OTHER ONLINE ASSHOLES: IGNORING, UNFRIENDING, AND BLOCKING

The nerds from multiple research labs who banded together to create the ARPANET (the forerunner to the Internet) in the 1960s and 1970s could not have imagined that their inventions would set the stage for a worldwide plague called "cyberbullying" — the wrenching and ridiculous online harassment that ranges from name-calling, to sexual harassment, to stalking, to physical threats. Indeed, a steady stream of such nastiness is now part of the territory for famous people. Even the most wholesome and innocent stars suffer through stretches where the insecure, vindictive, and often anonymous trolls rise up against them. That's what happened during the 2016 Olympics when gymnast and five-time gold medalist Gabby Douglas was labeled #CrabbyGabby and flamed on social media by thousands of people. She was left heartbroken and felt compelled to apologize for slights that were unintentional, trivial, and — in my view — nonexistent.

Gabby's mother Natalie Hawkins recounted her daughter's alleged sins to *Reuters:* "She's had to deal with people criticizing her hair, or people accusing her of bleaching her skin. They said she had breast enhancements, they said she wasn't smiling enough, she's unpatriotic."

People who aren't quite famous, but garner public attention, attract trolls too. Cambridge University historian Mary Beard is among the most intriguing and feisty targets, especially for sexist assholes. Beard is known for her popular books on the Roman Empire and strong opinions on topics including "the many ways that men have silenced outspoken women since the days of the ancients" — which she discusses in films, TV, and social media. As reported by *The New Yorker* in 2016, Beard has learned that women who "venture into traditional male territory" provoke online abuse. Beard observes that insults such as "shut up you bitch" are everyday fare and physical threats are remarkably common — such as the sick tweet one creep hurled at Beard, "I'm going to cut off your head and rape it."

There is plenty of quantitative evidence that online harassment is out of control. A 2014 survey of some three thousand U.S. adults by Pew Research found that 73% have witnessed others being harassed online and 40% have experienced it personally — for example, 27% of these Internet users reported being called offensive names and 7% reported being harassed for an extended period. Pew found that young adults eighteen to twenty-four years old were especially likely to experience harassment, which isn't surprising, as young adults are the heaviest users of social media. The research summary on Pew's website also reports that women in this age group were especially likely to experience the most severe forms of harassment: 25% were sexually harassed and 26% were stalked.

This nastiness happens because trolls hide behind anonymous screen names. But that's only part of the story. Much of the harassment uncovered in the Pew study was hurled at targets by friends, acquaintances, and people who use their real names on gaming sites, social media, and in emails and text messages. Many assholes who bashed and belittled Gabby Douglas and Mary Beard used real names online. And when *Wall Street Journal* reporter Elizabeth Bernstein did research for a story on cyberbullying, many of the victims who she interviewed knew their tormentors, including "a teacher who was cyberbullied by a student, a woman cyberbullied by neighbors upset about her dog, and a man who'd received more than 500 nasty texts in 48 hours from his ex-girlfriend."

The common denominator among all these purveyors of insults, disrespect, and hate is *a lack of eye contact with their targets* — which seems to be the main reason that online assholes feel so unfettered by the empathy, guilt, and plain old civility that might stop or slow their wrath during face-to-face interactions. For example, behavioral scientists Noam Lapidot-Lefler and Azy Barak at the University of Haifa assigned pairs of college students to engage in debates via text messages. These researchers examined multiple factors that could determine how nice or mean the students were to each other, including whether the students (who were strangers) spent time getting to know each other before starting the debate. Their main finding was that when students maintained eye contact during the debates, they made far fewer threats or other hostile comments—whether the duo had spent time getting to know each other beforehand (or not) didn't matter. So what do you do about online assholes? For starters, as with those jerks you face in person, many of the best solutions entail simply leaving ugly encounters rather than sticking around to throw their shit back at them. And if you are attacked by a certified asshole, end the relationship if you can. As *The New Yorker* reported in the story about Mary Beard, "There is even a Twitter account, @AvoidComments, which issues monitory statements: 'You wouldn't listen to someone named Bonerman26 in real life. Don't read the comments.'" Cyberbullying expert Patricia Wallace of the University of Maryland told the *Wall Street Journal*'s Elizabeth Bernstein that she advises victims to "unfriend, unfollow, unlink."

The Pew Research survey confirms that ignoring the jerks and ending relationships can be effective measures: 60% of those surveyed elected to ignore their most recent bullying incident, and most (over 80%) said it worked. Similar to Patricia Wallace's advice, the Pew survey found that other effective withdrawal tactics included unfriending or blocking the harasser, changing your username, deleting your online profile, withdrawing from the online interaction, and simply never returning to the upsetting online place.

That said, although it is more risky than ignoring or befriending online trolls and tormentors, confronting their nastiness does work sometimes. More than 20% of the victims interviewed by Pew did confront their abusers and most reported that doing so improved the situation. And historian Mary Beard has become a cult hero in some circles for battling online assholes: "The Troll Slayer" is how *The New Yorker* titled their story about her. One of Beard's many battles started when television critic A. A. Gill wrote a piece that attacked her physical appearance on a BBC show with insults including, "From behind she is 16; from the front, 60. The hair is a disaster, the outfit an embarrassment" and an admonishment that Beard "should be kept away from cameras altogether."

Beard fought back, belittling Gill's lack of education and arguing that "throughout Western history there have always been men like Gill who are frightened of smart women who speak their minds, and I guess, as a professor of classics at Cambridge University, I'm one of them." Beard won that round. Yet, as we've seen, and I'll show in more detail in chapter 6 on "Fighting Back," engaging in open warfare on assholes — be it offline or online — is risky and you best consider your relative power and exit options before launching an attack.

ON FIRING CLIENTS

A few years back, I got a note from a troubled executive at a professional services firm:

> Our clients are often the assholes. I am stuck with them because they literally pay our bills. These jerky people (whom I encounter ad nauseam at the highest levels in all Fortune 50 companies) sap the life out of our employees and make creating a sustainable, culturally viable environment difficult. How do I slow the carnage?

I exchanged emails with him and eventually gave a talk about assholes to the consultants at his company. In any business where you serve people, some customers and clients will be overbearing and difficult, and — as I discuss in later chapters — part of what makes for a skilled consultant, teacher, barista, or other service employee is the ability to deal with jerks in ways that calm them, protect your dignity and sanity, *and* still keep the money rolling in. I realized, however, after talking with leaders at this particular firm, that they had little, if any, history of firing their most abusive clients. This surprised me because my conversations and interviews with psychiatrists, priests, bartenders, hairstylists, film directors, lawyers, consultants, social workers, venture capitalists, CEOs, and people in many other occupations revealed they go to considerable lengths to avoid serving asshole clients and customers, and when they do get one, they often find ways to fire such jerks — or, sometimes, they get fired by the client on purpose.

In 2011, during a visit to Auckland, I heard a speech from Air New Zealand CEO Rob Fyfe, who led the company from 2005 to 2012 and is widely credited with turning around a dying airline — one that had been infamous for treating both employees and customers like dirt. Fyfe described how, after learning about a demanding (and very wealthy) customer who had hollered at and insulted his employees, Fyfe wrote the irate customer a letter informing him that it would no longer be possible for him to buy a ticket on Air New Zealand. Fyfe posted a copy of the letter on an internal website — with the banned passenger's name on it — for all his employees to see. Although Fyfe has since moved on, Air New Zealand still fires passengers who treat employees (or fellow passengers) with persistent and extreme disrespect. The company is doing a lot of other things well too. In 2016, Airlineratings.com selected Air New Zealand as the best airline in the world for the third year in a row.

I've have learned from wise people like Rob Fyfe that sometimes it's best to dump rude and overbearing clients who contact me about doing a speech or some consulting — or to create conditions where they fire me for not meeting their ridiculous demands. Let me give you an example: I once got a call two days before a long-planned talk from a consultant who had hired me to give a speech to executives from California wineries. I was looking forward to the speech because I love wine and winemakers, and rather than being paid money, my compensation would be in wine from a dozen or so excellent producers.

The consultant, however, demanded that I discard my planned topic and, instead, do a session on some pending legislation in California that would affect the wine industry. I explained that I knew nothing about the legislation, and if I tried to pretend, I would fail and the executives would get nothing from the session. She pushed, and pushed, and pushed — insisting that if I just studied the legislation for a day or so, I could figure out how to lead a three-hour session on it. As much as I was looking forward to the winemakers and the wine, I was curt and condescending when I informed her that I couldn't change to that topic and that she was setting both of us up for failure. She didn't want me any longer, and the feeling was mutual. Perhaps I should have been more gracious about it, but parting ways was the right thing to do.

Finally, to be realistic, financial considerations can and should affect which customers and clients you fire and which ones you tolerate. I love the rule of thumb used by the wine importer from Berkeley who wrote me, "In my business, we have a rule that says that a customer can either be an arsehole (I'm English originally) or a late pay, but not both. We have reduced stress considerably by excluding some customers on this basis."

FORESEE AND STEER CLEAR

It's better to avoid falling in with assholes in the first place than to run from them later (or worse, to get trapped and be unable to flee). Sure, it can be difficult to predict when you are about to fall in with jerks. You might do your homework, for example, by visiting Tripadvisor.com to pick a friendly hotel or restaurant, or studying Glassdoor or *Fortune*'s "100 Best Companies to Work For" list to choose a civilized and caring organization — and yet, even then, you can still get stuck with a certified asshole or hordes of them. Sometimes things start out great, but then some rude, selfish, or mean-spirited characters arrive, the poison spreads, and your world turns into a shit show. Other times, your once warm and supportive bosses or peers turn mean for reasons ranging from arrogance and insensitivity (that is stoked by success) to fear and status degradation that follows from being blamed for, or simply associated with, failure or scandal.

That said, you can save yourself much grief by doing some due diligence and searching for warning signs that "assholes are ahead" as you consider where to dine or stay, what church, golf club, or soccer club to join, where to work, or whether to take on that new client. Check out the accompanying "Asshole Detection Tips," which focus on warning signs to help you uncover and avert involvement with jerks. I especially want to put in a good word for what Wharton's Adam Grant described as "prosocial gossip" in the *Huffington Post* in 2013. Many of my tips entail seeking out gossip from reliable and caring allies. I am not talking about vicious, hateful, or false rumors. I mean well-founded concerns about bad people and places that can save you and others from being demeaned and damaged.

Professor Grant gives examples of how he's used such prosocial gossip, which I believe reflects well on him. Like the time he warned "a student to proceed cautiously when dealing with an adviser who has a history of exploiting students." Or when he gossiped about the "checkered history" of someone who a colleague was considering as a business partner. Grant prefers to say nice things about people. But he argues that negative — and well-founded — gossip is often justified: "I feel that I have a social responsibility to speak candidly. If I don't warn people about the most manipulative and Machiavellian marauders in their midst, I'm leaving them vulnerable to attack."

ASSHOLE DETECTION TIPS
Foresee and Steer Clear of Jerks

1. **Sure, Google them.** Check respected sources of ratings and rankings. But beware that Glassdoor's list of the 10 worst workplaces or *Fortune*'s list of the "100 Best Companies to Work For" aren't necessarily likely to match the experience you will have with any particular department, group, person, or client.
2. **Reliable gossip is gold.** Who do you know who works with them now or has in the past? What can they tell you about the people and the place in general, and what insight do they have about the particular work you will do and people you will deal with?
3. **Past victims or enemies?** Seek out those people who left because they were unhappy or got fired in particular. If they worked with the group or person you are considering, the information will be especially instructive.

4. **Exposure to other assholes?** Have they worked with or been trained by known assholes? That's a red flag. Assholes attract and breed more assholes.

5. **Bad first impression?** When you exchange emails, messages, or early phone calls, are you getting any hints that they might be jerks?

6. **Bad second impression?** During initial meetings or interviews, how do they treat you? Do they make you feel respected? Do they care? Or do they already show signs of being hostile, rude, or overly demanding? Things will only get worse.

7. **Damn with faint praise?** Listen carefully to how underlings and peers talk about people in power. After all, if you are a stranger, they aren't likely to bash their bosses or teammates. Do they say the right words . . . but without a hint of warmth or excitement? Do they change the subject quickly when you ask about leaders or other powerful people? Anything short of total enthusiasm is a red flag.

8. **Signs of a superiority complex?** Listen carefully to how people in power talk about others. Is everyone else a jerk, idiot, traitor, or loser? Do they seem to bad-mouth or be dismissive of just about everyone except for those who kiss up to them?

9. **How do they treat each other?** How do people with more power treat those with less? Watch how peers interact — is it a *Lord of the Flies* situation? Beware of aggressive teasing, rude interruptions, pained facial expressions, and glum silence.

10. **All transmission and no reception?** Use two diagnostic questions proposed by my Stanford colleague Huggy Rao to help determine if people are self-absorbed:
    - How much do your potential superiors, colleagues, or clients dominate the talking time? Do they let you or anyone else get a word in edgewise?
    - What is the ratio of questions that people ask versus statements they make? If they never ask any questions, and just bark out orders, show off their knowledge, and don't have much interest in what others say, that's a bad sign.
11. **A toe in the water?** Can you start with a small commitment rather than a big one? A small project for a client or perhaps an internship or trial period? That way, you can learn if there is an asshole problem before you sign up for the long term.

One of my relatives who has dealt with and dodged overbearing and sometimes crazy assholes for over twenty-five years relies on many of these "Asshole Detection Tips." She does freelance work that involves organizing complex projects that cost millions of dollars for wealthy clients, many of whom are billionaires (sorry, I best keep the details vague for the sake of family harmony). She has made a good living at this work for a long time and is known for completing projects on time and on budget, meeting exacting standards, and being adept at dealing with her clients' quirks, moods, impatience, and insistence on perfection (even when they are unwilling to pay the steep price).

Many of her clients are wonderful and "really fun" — but there are also certain types who she avoids at all costs. She has learned the hard way that some of the most selfish and cruel clients surround themselves with ass-kissing supplicants that they treat like dirt. And some of the worst add an extra twist: they take perverse pleasure in insisting that project managers like her commit to timetables and budgets that are impossible to meet — and then berate and bad-mouth them when the project begins to fail, even when the project manager had warned them that their goals were impossible to achieve (and the client insisted on charging forward despite the expert advice).

She has learned that it's best to part ways with clients who are too cruel or crazy. And she has learned to spot which people will be hell to work for, so she quits (and gets fired) less often now than when her radar was less well-honed. She checks with other people in her business before agreeing to meet with, let alone work for, a potential client: this exchange of reliable gossip is essential for avoiding known assholes. And when she meets with a potential client, she looks for signs that he or she mistreats other project managers, assistants, maintenance workers, construction crews, and anyone else on the payroll. No matter how warm and charming the potential client might be to her, it's a red flag that she has learned to heed.

Just recently, she met with a billionaire about a potential project and "noticed a particular behavior." He was "dismissive but not abusive toward low-wage workers with minimum skills who were loyal to him and worked tirelessly for him." But it was the more skilled workers, the highly paid ones (like my relative) who were "the subject of constant abuse and under threat of termination and replacement by a lower-wage worker." This billionaire continues to court my relative to work for him, and to join him for dinner to talk about future projects. But she "always politely refuses" because she knows that if they start working together, he would treat her like those other victims at some point.

Along similar lines, when you are interviewing for a new job, don't just focus on how you are treated; be sure to watch how your potential boss and colleagues treat others. One candidate who interviewed to be a manufacturing manager wrote me that he was wary because his potential boss had spent years at another company known for breeding incompetent assholes. So, during the interview, the candidate decided "to see how he interacted with shop floor employees and the people who worked directly for him, to see how he spoke to them, and his verbal and visual actions." The candidate noticed people on the floor stood far away as the boss addressed them, that "he never smiled, and no one smiled at him," and "he passed people on the line without so much as a nod." The candidate's interactions with the boss were even worse: "He cut me off TWICE when I was talking like I wasn't even speaking, and then once even rudely didn't even PRETEND to listen to me as I talked about my background." He got the offer but turned it down because, he wrote, "I believe in my heart, I would have ended up working for an asshole."

WHAT YOU DO VERSUS HOW YOU DO IT

By fleeing from assholes or—better still—detecting and declining to engage with them, you can spare yourself, your friends, and your colleagues much heartbreak. I love those "take this job and shove it" stories. And as that engineer who used the "Kamikaze Method" to quit and take the boss down with him illustrates, making a strategic stink can work on special occasions. Certainly, some assholes are so vile and unrepentant that they deserve all the bad-mouthing, unflattering press, and lawsuits they get.

Take former American Apparel CEO Dov Charney. According to a *Los Angeles Times* story in June of 2015, court documents alleged that Charney's bad behavior included calling accounting employees "Filipino pigs . . . with your faces in the trough," attempting to strangle an employee "with his hands and rub dirt into his face," and storing "footage on company equipment of himself having sex with models." Charney's alleged misdeeds weren't a new story. Back in 2008, the *Los Angeles Times* reported a lawsuit against Charney that alleged he called staffers "sluts" and "whores" and had invited a female employee to "masturbate in front of him." American Apparel's lawyers claimed that his behavior led the company to "incur nearly $10 million in litigation costs." Charney has denied all of these allegations, but when he tried to sue his former company for defamation, Superior Court judge Terry Green blocked the suit and, according to a *Litigation Daily* story in October of 2015, the judge blasted back, "You know, I think there's a greater likelihood that I'll be the first American astronaut stranded on Mars" than Charney could win the suit. Judge Green added that Charney's alleged misconduct was "so far over the top that you can't see the top anymore."

More often, however, you and those you leave behind (even the assholes you spurn) will be better off if you can depart in calm, considerate, and discreet ways that enable everyone to save face. So when you quit a job or dump a client, try to give them some advance notice, finish your work if possible, and make a smooth handoff so that you don't leave others in the lurch. That way you won't burn bridges you might need later. It's also dangerous to confront or bad-mouth the jerks you jilt because, after all, they are assholes and thus prone to being vindictive. They not only may take out their anger on you via backstabbing and bad recommendations; they may exact revenge on the friends and allies that you leave behind.

That is why *Forbes* writer Susan Adams suggests that, even if you are leaving a job or boss you hate, it's safer to keep your parting message short and sweet. And if your boss or HR asks why you are leaving, even if you aim to explain the "asshole problem" in the most calm and balanced way, beware that narcissistic and Machiavellian people are thin-skinned. They are prone to lash out at, blame, and try to screw anyone who doesn't flatter and kiss up to them. So you might be better off keeping things upbeat, brief, and vague — and just get the hell out.

Here's the upshot. When you take actions that may offend, hurt, or threaten others — whether those on the receiving end are assholes or treasured colleagues — *"there is a big difference between what you do and how you do it."* That expression always makes me think of my friend Michael Dearing. He is a no-nonsense businessperson: one of his favorite sayings is "capitalism is a self-cleaning oven." Michael has left jobs at places including Disney and eBay, fired people in major roles at those and other places, and these days — as a venture capitalist who has helped launch more than a hundred companies — he has removed CEOs and pulled the plug on failing companies. In fact, Michael taught at Stanford with several colleagues and me for years, and eventually left us too!

Yet Michael is beloved by almost everyone he has quit working with (including me), has fired, or stopped funding. It's because of the WAY in which he does it. He treats people with respect and remains emotionally supportive both during and after the separation. When working with great colleagues ("95% of the time") or the occasional asshole ("5% or less"), Michael told me that he designs the "how" part of his actions "with the other person's point of view in mind." Even when breaking off with an asshole, he works to "convey the truth in respectful and empathetic ways."

Sure, Michael has made a few enemies along the way and, looking back, he wonders if he could have been warmer and more understanding with them. That's how Michael is; he is given to blame himself rather than others — even when they are likely at fault. He understands the virtues of being slow to label others as assholes, and being quick to label yourself as one.

4 Asshole Avoidance Techniques

REDUCING YOUR EXPOSURE

"DON'T ENGAGE with crazy."

That's what Katy said when I asked for her best asshole survival advice. I am talking about Dr. Katy DeCelles of the University of Toronto, an academic hotshot who studies abusive people and ugly conflict, including that research on outbursts by basketball coaches discussed in chapter 2, the cruelty (as well as apathy and caring) expressed between prison guards and inmates, air rage incidents, and "fights before flights" — where passengers heap abuse on airline employees at the boarding gate.

Katy's warning is a good starting place for anyone who is troubled, tormented, or hurt by jerks. All of us sometimes get trapped in (or decide to endure) encounters and relationships with assholes — where our goal is to just survive the ugliness the best we can. In Katy's language, this chapter is about — when you can't or won't avert engaging with crazy completely — how to limit the frequency, duration, and intensity of the abuse you face and feel.

I focus on reducing the amount of exposure because jerks are a lot like sick people who are infected with a dangerous and contagious disease. We human beings "catch" many of our thoughts, emotions, and behaviors from others (even when we don't want to). Becoming "infected" changes us (usually for the worse), and we pass our negative germs along to others (even if we don't intend to). Evidence that negative emotions and behavior are contagious was strong when I wrote *The No Asshole Rule*, and it's far stronger now. A 2013 summary of workplace aggression research led by M. Sandy Hershcovis of the University of Manitoba reports numerous new studies on how abusive supervisors, peers, and customers, and workplaces that are hostile and unfair, infect employees so that they — in turn — treat others like dirt.

Demeaning and disrespectful behavior seeps into other relationships with innocent bystanders: Abused employees tend to mistreat family members, not just colleagues and customers. Bad feelings spread in the classroom too; research from the University of British Columbia suggests there is "stress contagion" between teachers and elementary school students. Teachers suffering from "burnout," or feelings of emotional exhaustion, had students with higher cortisol levels — which are linked to learning and mental health problems. And a 2015 study by Trevor Foulk and his colleagues from the University of Florida shows that even a single exposure to a rude person (e.g., a mildly insulting email from a customer) can turn a person into a "carrier," who in turn infects others with the negative behavior — so it spreads much "like the common cold."

KEEP YOUR DISTANCE

Here's how a small band of university administrators reduced their exposure — and that of many others — to the local certified asshole. About fifteen years ago, I knew a professor from a prestigious university who received a large research grant. He began pounding his tenured chest, berating administrators about how much money he brought in, how prestigious he was, and how much space he would need to house his team. The administrators — and most other professors and staff members he worked with — were tired of his arrogance and personal attacks. So they conjured up a brilliant solution: they offered him a new suite of offices several miles away from the main campus. The pompous professor took the bait. He was delighted to have so much space; his colleagues were even more pleased because they now rarely saw or heard from him after he moved to his new digs.

That story is instructive because it shows, when it comes to assholes, it's sometimes wise to add rather than remove communication barriers — and physical distance is one of the most protective barriers. You might be surprised by how much relief comes from putting just a few extra feet between you and your tormentors.

In the 1970s, MIT professor Tom Allen showed that the closer people sat to one another, the more frequently they communicated — not just face-to-face communication, but via all media including telephone calls. Subsequent studies on the "Allen curve" or "the law of propinquity" confirm that people are four times more likely to communicate regularly with a colleague who sits six feet away compared to one who sits sixty feet away. Employees rarely communicate with colleagues on separate floors or in separate buildings; in fact, once people are about 150 feet away, communication becomes so rare that a pair of coworkers might as well be in different cities or countries. You might think the rise of the Internet would end this "out of sight, out of mind" effect. But studies by researchers including Professor David Krackhardt of Carnegie Mellon and CEO Ben Waber of Sociometric Solutions find that people who work on the same floor, and especially, who sit close together, are still far more likely to engage in daily communication of all kinds, including via email, texts, and social media.

The Allen curve has direct implications for asshole management. If you can ship the local asshole to another building, or even just twenty or thirty more feet away, you can reduce your distress and risk of infection. And this research suggests that when those university administrators enticed that obnoxious professor to move across town, it was just as effective as sending him to another country. If you can't ship out your colleague, try to move yourself. While switching to another floor or building is best, putting even a little physical distance between you and that toxic person helps a lot.

"Workforce scientist" Dr. Michael Housman and his colleagues studied the "spillover effects" that are triggered when different types of employees sit close to each other. They tracked two thousand workers at a large technology company for two years. In 2016, Housman told *Fast Company* that they discovered a "toxic density" effect: much like research that shows rudeness spreads like a common cold, they found that sitting near a destructive jerk dramatically increases a worker's risk of infection. Housman explained, "If you add a toxic worker to within a 25-foot radius of a focal worker, the chance that the focal worker becomes a toxic worker themselves more than doubles (112.5% increase)." Housman even found that sitting with a bunch of contagious assholes can get you fired: "Employees are 150% more likely to be terminated for toxic behavior when sitting in a toxic employee-dense seating area."

This "defense by distance" tactic applies to where you sit in public places and meetings too. If you are seated near rude or wasted jerks at a movie or restaurant, on an airplane, a bus, or a plane, do what you can to move away from them and their hostile shenanigans. And putting distance between you and known assholes can help you survive social gatherings, political fund-raisers, volunteer organizations, the workplace, or other places where you attend meetings.

Last year, I met a crusty and charming engineer who was quite proud of surviving fifteen tough years at Apple. One secret to his success was keeping his distance from the late Steve Jobs. This engineer reported that — although Jobs did mellow with age — it wasn't just a myth: He was one of many at Apple who avoided getting in the elevator with Jobs because he didn't want to get interrogated or end up working late for weeks or months. And he explained that when his team met with Jobs, he avoided sitting near him because "the closer you were to Jobs, the more likely that something bad would happen to you."

DUCKING STRATEGIES

Of course, sometimes you can't avoid interactions with assholes. But if you are thoughtful — even a bit sneaky — you can limit how often and long you are subjected to their poison. That's what Pamela Lutgen-Sandvik from North Dakota State University found in her studies of workplace bullies. The victims that Pam interviewed called this "ducking" and many practiced it as "nearly an art form." A vice president at a sports fishing business, for example, worked for an owner in an all-glass office where the "constant surveillance was deliberate" and where "he'd scream and yell every day." The vice president said, "Veins would pop out of his head; he'd spit, he'd point, he'd threaten daily, all day long to anyone in his way, every day that I was there." She limited exposure by staying out of the office as much as possible: "You learn not to show up at work too much. You make arrangements to go to meetings. You're just too busy to go to the office."

Ducking strategies are especially useful for navigating long-term predicaments. Such strategies have sure helped me. For years, I was stuck with a colleague who I believed was mean-spirited and narcissistic. It made me ill to attend the meetings she led. I found one-on-one conversations with her to be even more painful. She was so self-absorbed that, as one of my fellow professors pointed out, while she always started informal conversations by first asking about you, she rarely made it to the two-minute mark without shifting all conversation to the many ways in which she was so marvelous.

I had never met anyone who bragged so much. I was disgusted by her constant talk about how powerful she was, all the important people she knew, her remarkable productivity and impact, and how generally superior she was to the rest of us. In my opinion, she was also a world-class backstabber—relentlessly belittling, bad-mouthing, and undermining rivals, critics, and anyone else she saw as a threat to her prestige and power. I did everything I could to avoid those horrible one-on-one conversations. I also avoided as many meetings as I could whenever she led them. Unfortunately, I couldn't miss them all.

But when her behavior made me sick (a nausea akin to seasickness) or I felt an outburst coming on, I often left meetings early (I did this at least twenty times). And I didn't explain why. It seemed better to say nothing than to lie. I eventually learned that other colleagues used similar tactics. Some reduced their exposure to her toxins by arriving very late to her meetings; I couldn't bring myself to do that because my mother raised me to be obsessive about arriving on time to everything (even though it isn't always the best strategy). For me, fleeing the scene early and often helped save my sanity.

SLOW THE RHYTHM

Dealing with assholes can be like having a new puppy. When you scream "No!" as he chews on your expensive new shoes, it isn't taken as a punishment. True, you're upset about the shoes, but that puppy loves the attention. Your screaming just encourages more bad behavior, and next thing you know — as my dog Bugsy did to me — that cute little mutt has destroyed your $400 pair of glasses and a black pen that explodes all over the light beige carpet. Some assholes take a similar kind of pleasure in your pain. When they do something that generates a strong reaction from you — be it obsequious ass-kissing, effusive apologizing, trembling with fear, giving in to tears or anger, or sending that long and carefully worded email you spent an hour crafting in response to their imaginary emergency — the pleasure centers in their twisted minds light up.

Consider a brain scanning study by University of Chicago psychologist Benjamin Lahey and his colleagues. They compared adolescents with "aggressive conduct disorder" (e.g., histories of stealing, lying, vandalizing, and bullying) with a control group of otherwise similar kids who lacked such history. When the researchers showed the bullies pictures of people who were experiencing pain — for example, from a hammer dropped on a toe — the pleasure regions of their brains lit up (this did not happen to the kids in the control group). Lahey told *National Geographic* in 2008, "We think it means that they like seeing people in pain" and "they are getting positively reinforced every time they bully and are aggressive to other people."

The researchers emphasize that their findings are tentative — but Internet trolls do appear to enjoy similar sick pleasures. As veteran online community manager Jessamyn West told the *Guardian* in 2016, "Trolling is crafted by people who believe it is their job to figure out exactly what people's buttons are, then press those buttons." The same seems to go for bullies in the schoolyard and the workplace — your obvious pain is their pleasure, and each time they provoke it, they are reinforced to torment you more and more.

As I said in chapter 3, it's often best just to ignore or to break off with such assholes. Alas, that isn't always possible. But figuring how to slow the rhythm of exchanges as much as possible — and how to delay and deny your tormentor as much reinforcement as possible — can help you endure and even reform such jerks. A former doctoral student who was plagued by an abusive, temperamental, and irrationally demanding advisor explained to me how she navigated this tension by using "slow down" tactics to survive several difficult years. At first, when her advisor sent her demeaning emails, or called at an inappropriate time (e.g., 2 a.m.) to rant at and criticize the student, she jumped up and responded right away. This fueled even more abuse because her advisor got the attention he wanted, which in turn reinforced his bad behavior — just as with those teenage bullies in Professor Lahey's experiment, the pleasure centers in his brain lit up. The student learned to respond more and more slowly over the years, first taking hours, then days, and then sometimes weeks before sending a reply. Even when the advisor sent her a batch of obnoxious and insulting emails, the student waited two or three days, and sometimes longer, to read them all at once. Then she sent a single measured response. Over time, while the advisor never became less abusive, he sent fewer and fewer emails, and called less often and during more civilized times.

Another advantage of delay was that the student had time to calm down — to quell the temptation to respond with nastiness in kind — which helped her avoid a vicious circle of escalating insults and accusations. This PhD student used a similar tactic for scheduling regular face-to-face meetings: she slowly and steadily "trained" her mean-spirited mentor to shift from weekly, to biweekly, and finally to monthly meetings. This student, now a tenured professor at a prestigious university, believes that she would never have finished her PhD, found a great job, or kept her sanity without these and many other tricks that limited exposure to her "bat shit crazy advisor." This "rhythm method" can help anyone besieged by such micromanaging pleasure seekers: try to slow things down, make THEM squirm and suffer as much as you can, and train them to back off and wait. They might just stop badgering you — and turn their attention to more responsive and thus more satisfying targets instead.

Slowing the rhythm is also useful during interactions with abusive clients and customers. In the 1990s, I did an ethnographic study of telephone bill collectors where I was trained as a collector, spent a week making collection calls to debtors who were late on Master-Card and Visa payments, and then spent months observing and interviewing the real collectors. We were taught that the more irate the debtor — the more he or she screamed, swore, and insulted us — the more long pauses we should take before answering questions and the more slowly and calmly we should talk. A supervisor instructed me, "If you talk softer and softer and softer, they're going to have to stop to listen or they're not going to hear anything you're saying. The louder you get, the louder they get. And if you start to tone it down, they start to tone it down."

The best collectors were masterful at changing the rhythm and tone of even the most abusive, insulting, and mean-spirited debtors. I listened to numerous calls where a debtor would yell at a skilled collector for a minute or more, then the collector would pause awhile and then talk slowly and calmly (and use soothing words), the debtor would yell some more, the collector would speak slowly, softly, and calmly again, and so on. In ten minutes or less, most debtors would calm down and be nicer. They often apologized, made the late payment, or both.

HIDE IN PLAIN SIGHT

One way that assholes leave others feeling disrespected and demeaned is to ignore them as people. That is, to treat them as if they were invisible. A classic crappy move is to treat someone like a piece of furniture that you use but do not acknowledge as a human being — no eye contact, no smile, no thanks, no connection of any sort.

Yet invisibility is a double-edged sword. It provides protection because sometimes attracting a jerk's attention is even worse than being ignored. Some assholes notice you only when they believe that you've done something wrong or offensive. Or they are agitated, anxious, insecure, or depressed for other reasons — and you serve as a convenient scapegoat for their built-up bile. That's why people who are knee-deep in assholes (or stuck with one or two) can benefit from mastering the art of being there but going unnoticed by potential tormentors.

It's a bit like those animals that turn the same color and shape as their surroundings to hide in plain sight from predators. Like arctic foxes whose coats turn white when it snows and then brown or gray to match the summer tundra. Or "decorator crabs" that attach seaweed, algae, rocks, or sponges to their bodies as camouflage. People who want to be invisible to assholes use different kinds of camouflage, but it helps them blend into the background too. They are quiet when others talk. They are boring when others are interesting.

They try to do work that is neither lousy nor excellent, but somewhere in the middle. They dress to avoid standing out — just like everyone else, but with a bit less pizzazz. They hide behind bland and blank expressions. Their aim is to lay low and to not make waves, to be invisible and forgettable.

Consider the airport security screening process. It sucks. It's usually crowded and loud; you are surrounded with harried and unhappy people; rules are strictly enforced yet often confusing; strangers dig through your most private possessions; people poke, prod, and frisk you; and you risk being delayed, detained, and perhaps incarcerated. If skilled sadists wanted to design an experience to breed temporary assholes, they would be hard-pressed to come up with something worse than what the U.S. Transportation Security Administration (TSA) is required to do to passengers. Of course, from the other perspective, the transportation security officers (TSOs) employed by TSA must deal with a lot of assholes. Not only do they face an endless parade of often pissed-off passengers; they work under intense surveillance by their TSA superiors who insist that they follow precise rules and procedures, keep the line moving, and be civil (or at least not rude) to passengers.

Harvard Business School researchers Michel Anteby and Curtis Chan interviewed eighty-nine TSA employees in 2011 to learn about how their work was organized, the pressures that TSOs felt, and how TSOs dealt with this simultaneously distressing and boring work. Anteby and Chan found that a hallmark of TSOs' work was that they were seen but unnoticed. TSA managers watched what TSOs did closely (managers observed them directly and watched video monitors linked to six or seven surveillance cameras in the screening area). And supervisors often stepped in to correct or to help TSOs. Yet despite this intensive surveillance, Anteby and Chan found that the TSA managers focused far less attention on TSOs as individuals or on how they felt. TSOs were often seen by management, and saw themselves, as "invisible and interchangeable workers monitoring a similarly invisible and interchangeable mass of travelers" who just disappeared "into the woodwork."

Anteby and Chan learned that many TSOs viewed such "invisibility" as a good thing and played an active role in "getting disappeared." Being noticed often meant trouble—it was followed by reprimands, being assigned to difficult and emotionally demanding roles, written warnings from management, temporary suspensions, or even getting fired. So TSOs devised ways to "hide in plain sight" and to "float under the radar." They used ducking strategies including taking extra breaks when things were slow and going to the bathroom as often as possible. Although, in theory, TSOs changed positions every thirty minutes to break up the boredom, some TSOs learned to linger in those areas that—while still visible to passengers—involve less interaction and a bit more distance from them. For example, being a "pat-down officer" who touches and searches passengers requires close and uncomfortable contact with passengers—who Anteby and Chan report were annoyed and sometimes lashed out in anger. In contrast, the "X-ray viewing task" is insulated from passengers—that's the TSO who looks at the monitor to see if there is something suspicious in your luggage. As one explained, "You do get a little break from the public when you're on X-ray because you don't have to deal with them at all."

Other invisibility strategies used by TSOs involved downplaying "their selfhood." Some TSOs avoided doing excellent work because they felt that being noticed as an individual rather than as an anonymous cog in the machine carried too many other risks. Others avoided talking with supervisors and fellow TSOs about their private lives to remain as just another anonymous and interchangeable TSO rather than an interesting person. Still others pretended not to pay attention to conversations about work or personal matters among supervisors or passengers to help ensure they weren't noticed and were left alone. Anteby and Chan found that TSOs did sometimes try to draw attention to themselves; for example, some bragged about the positive "comment cards" they received from passengers who praised their professionalism. But the risks of garnering attention were considerable, in part, because TSOs found it difficult to perform well consistently.

As Anteby and Chan point out, people who fear retribution from the powerful have long used invisibility as a protective cloak. This theme runs through academic and journalistic accounts of other occupations including assembly-line workers, engineers, food servers, nurses, and cops. And sometimes — if you are observant and patient — being invisible gives you access to information that can help you turn the tables on powerful assholes. For example, in the early 1990s, Charlie Galunic (now a professor at INSEAD business school in France) and I did a fascinating interview with Bob Demmons, who was among the few African Americans in the San Francisco Fire Department when he was hired in 1974. Although Demmons was trained to fight fires, he was soon assigned to be the driver for the department chief — a demeaning job stereotypically reserved for African Americans. In that role, Demmons visited every firehouse in the city many times. He also was privy to numerous conversations where the chief and many other powerful city officials simply forgot that Demmons was present as they talked about sensitive issues and sometimes suspect actions.

Demmons was much like the main character in Ralph Ellison's classic 1950s novel *Invisible Man,* where an African American man's race rendered him socially invisible to others. When Charlie and I interviewed Demmons, he said serving as the chief's driver rankled him, but it also eventually helped him and other minorities and women. He learned and heard many things about the San Francisco Fire Department from powerful people who forgot he was present — including a lot of dirt — that helped him become an effective leader in a long battle against discrimination in the department. Ultimately, as head of the Black Firefighters Association, Demmons played a key role in the lawsuits that struck down racist hiring policies and led to court-ordered integration of the department. And, in 1996, Demmons became San Francisco's first African American fire chief.

Demmons's story reveals the complexity of being present but unseen. It bruised his dignity to be treated as the invisible man who drove the fire chief around San Francisco. Yet because people in power often forgot he was there, Demmons learned lessons that enabled him to gain influence — and, ultimately, win the battle for justice against those who treated him and other minorities like dirt (not just African Americans). His actions set the stage for bringing more women, Asian, and Hispanic firefighters into the department.

HUMAN SHIELDS

The idea here is to find or to recruit "blockers" who are able, willing, and even delighted to take abuse that would otherwise be heaped on you. There are many roles where taking heat from assholes and other difficult people comes with the territory. As I wrote in *Good Boss, Bad Boss*, although abuse, interruptions, confusion, and other shit often roll down hierarchies, most organizations are also designed so that it's management's job to protect "the core work of the organization from uncertainty and external perturbations." This means that "a good boss takes pride in serving as a human shield, absorbing and deflecting heat from superiors and customers, doing all manner of boring and silly tasks, and battling back against every idiot and slight that makes life unfair or harder than necessary on his or her charges."

So you can reduce your own exposure by finding bosses with the will and skill to protect their charges from assholes and idiots. To illustrate, the CEO isn't really the top dog in most companies and nonprofits. He or she reports to a board of directors. Good CEOs protect employees, customers, and investors from jerks on the board. Recall the Silicon Valley CEO that I quoted at the outset of chapter 1, the one who asked about dealing with clueless and mean-spirited board members ("boardholes") and boards with numerous nasty directors ("doucheboards")? We met for a glass of wine to talk about that challenge. At a previous company where he was also CEO, he had a pompous and pushy boardhole who he called "the idea man." This director was constantly proposing new ideas on everything from business strategies, to HR practices, to tweaks and massive changes in products. He often demanded that the CEO's senior team implement his ideas or at least devote considerable time to evaluating them — even though doing so would create unnecessary distractions and stress throughout the company. And in the CEO's opinion, most of the idea man's ideas were terrible. The CEO did occasionally implement some of this jerk's better and less intrusive ideas ("an occasional juicy bone to placate him"), but he routinely deflected, stalled, and when necessary argued with the boardhole. To protect his people's mental health and the company's performance, he especially ignored or deflected most of the idea man's requests for one-on-one meetings with employees. That's the kind of human shield that you want on your side.

Similarly, I exchanged multiple emails with the director of sports medicine at a big university who took pride in protecting his people from rude and vindictive senior administrators. He said something wise about what it takes to be an effective shield: "I always tell the people who work for me the same thing: My job is to hold the umbrella so the shit from above doesn't hit you. Your job is to keep me from having to use it." As I wrote in the *Harvard Business Review* in 2010, "he picked his fights carefully—because if he developed the reputation as a chronic complainer, or worse, got fired —he would be unable to protect anyone. So he asked his followers to avoid bending or breaking misguided university rules and procedures, or upsetting university officials, unless doing so was essential to their performance or dignity."

Bosses aren't the only ones charged with facing and absorbing heat from mean-spirited colleagues, customers, students, parishioners, reporters, constituents, or donors. Companies, government agencies, work and sports teams, and online groups appoint and recruit members—and sometimes outsiders—to serve as human shields. Author Tom Wolfe wrote about the protective powers of dull civil servants that he dubbed "flak catchers"—how they took the heat from, screened, and cooled down irate and intimidating constituents who barged in and insisted on meeting with San Francisco city supervisors. As Paul Friedman from the University of Kansas put it, flak catchers are "lightning rods" and "hassle handlers" who take and absorb "jolts sent by the dissatisfied." Taking such heat is part of the job for receptionists; executive assistants; security guards; spokespersons for companies, universities, and political campaigns; people who work in complaint departments; and bouncers.

Skilled dental hygienists also play this role. A 2013 study of nearly two thousand Finnish dentists found that when they worked in close cooperation with their dental assistants, dentists suffered less pressure to present fake emotions to their patients and performed their jobs better. Part of the reason, the researchers suggest, is that a skilled dental assistant (who usually sees patients before the dentist and often sees them more frequently) can "buffer" the dentist from difficult and demanding patients. In other words, they take the patient's flak and cool them out, which spares dentists from having to deal with it.

"Hassle handling" is a more explicit part of other roles. I interviewed a Disney executive (he asked to remain anonymous) who described the employees, or "cast members," in guest relations at Disneyland as "full-time asshole handlers," a tall order given that Disneyland's official tagline is "The Happiest Place on Earth." When a guest is rude, angry, swearing loudly, or visibly upset, cast members not only try to calm him or her; they are adept at reducing the exposure of other guests to such un-Disney malice and misery. The executive emphasized that cast members are taught that separating unhappy guests from others is crucial because negative emotions are so contagious. Cast members nudge upset and irate guests to talk with them in less-crowded nooks and crannies of the park; guests who become especially unhinged are led into a "cool-down room" in City Hall on Disneyland's Main Street — so they can discuss concerns, vent, and compose themselves without contaminating others (City Hall also houses the complaint department — so it is probably the unhappiest place at Disneyland).

Finally, you might collaborate with peers to alternate between roles that involve high versus low exposure to assholes — that way, in the words of the Rolling Stones, you each get your "fair share of abuse" (and relief from it). Sometimes, trading places is baked into standard operating procedures — but be wary of those procedures that are unfair, especially to you! Recall that, in the research on transportation security officers by Michel Anteby and Curtis Chan, the policy was to rotate TSOs between different positions every thirty minutes — both to decrease boredom and because some jobs (such as patting down passengers) entailed getting up close and personal with passengers in ways that annoyed and sometimes angered them. Alas, Anteby and Chan's research also revealed that female TSOs were assigned to difficult and asshole-intensive roles (especially pat-down tasks) more often than male TSOs — and supervisors sometimes punished women who tried to take extra time to recover. So beware of joining, supporting, or designing unfair systems that tend to provide far more relief to some targets than to others.

You also can make informal agreements with others so that everybody gets (more or less) their fair share of abuse. Numerous lawyers, accountants, and management consultants have told me that they take turns dealing with difficult clients. (One consultant remarked to me, "Well, it's my night to sit next to our big client and all-star asshole at dinner.") Similarly, restaurant workers alternate exposure to customers who are bad tippers, or hyperdemanding, or rude. When I worked at a now-defunct pizza parlor in Palo Alto called The MBJ Ranch Room in my late teens, an obnoxious drunk known as "Crazy Mary" came in most nights at about 8 p.m. She swore, ranted, and spit while she talked. It took her forever to order her food and then she usually complained about it — the serving was too small, it was too expensive, or the pizza had too much sauce. None of us wanted to serve Crazy Mary, but someone had to. My co-worker Arnie came up with a fair solution; when she walked in, the two or three of us in the kitchen played a quick game of rock-paper-scissors; the loser took Mary's order and dealt with her complaints that night.

SAFETY ZONES

The renowned sociologist Erving Goffman portrayed everyday life as akin to the theater, where we all have roles — public "presentations of self" — to perform; but, also like the theater, there are "backstage regions" where we can prepare for, hide from, and recover from the demands and distress of our more public, or onstage, performances. People who "perform" roles of all kinds use "backstage regions" to reduce their exposure to assholes and other distressing characters, to prepare for and recover from encounters, and to give and receive support to fellow targets.

For example, the "nurses' lounge" serves all these functions. When my colleague Dan Denison and I spent a week observing and interviewing operating room nurses in a Michigan hospital, what we saw and heard dovetailed with research that suggests nurses are one of the most intensely bullied occupations. They are blamed, insulted, pressured, and belittled from every direction — the flak comes from patients, patients' families, fellow nurses, hospital administrators, and, of course, physicians (especially surgeons). The nurses that we studied were belittled and sexually harassed — as I said in *The No Asshole Rule,* we dubbed one surgeon "Dr. Gooser" after we observed him chasing a female nurse down the hall while he tried to pinch her behind. Right after that incident, Dan and I tried to follow several nurses into their lounge to talk to them about Dr.

Gooser and other matters. They made clear to us that *no one* was allowed in the lounge except nurses — no doctors, no administrators, and certainly no researchers.

Backstage regions are sometimes dedicated private areas like that nurses' lounge. Examples include the teachers' lounge where educators find relief and recovery from students; "greenrooms" (which aren't usually green) where television guests and other performers are separated from audiences; and that "cool-down room" at Disneyland's City Hall — which fits Goffman's theatrical analogy especially well. Disney labels the places where "guests" visit as "onstage" areas. When "onstage," the "cast members" such as janitors and ride operators and "performers" such as Mickey Mouse and Snow White are required to stay in character; they are only allowed to eat, joke with coworkers, and such — in effect, to act out of character — when they are "backstage." And while most "backstage" regions are reserved for Disney employees, the "cool-down room" is an exception.

The "crying rooms" that guests can rent at the Mitsui Garden Hotel Yotsuya in Tokyo is an especially explicit — and strange — example of a space dedicated to relief and recovery from assholes and other problems. These rooms are designed to be safe havens for young female guests to "de-stress" by "bawling their eyes out." That's what a hotel spokesperson told *Time* in 2015; for about 85 U.S. dollars, these special rooms are "stocked with tissues, 'warm eye masks' and about a dozen sentimental movies."

Other "backstage" areas aren't dedicated as "safety zones" but are used for that purpose. The local coffee shop or bar often provides a safe refuge from all manner of workplace assholes. Hallways, fire escapes, and the water cooler also serve as backstage regions. A friend who is a pilot tells me that, on long flights, flight attendants sometimes join her and the copilot in the cockpit, in part, to get a few minutes of relief from passengers (and often to vent about some asshole who is drunk, demanding special treatment, or engaging in borderline sexual harassment).

Smoke breaks not only provide people a nicotine fix; they often serve as makeshift backstage gatherings that provide relief and release from the local assholes. For example, I worked with Stanford PhD student Joachim Lyon, who did in-depth ethnographies of two design firms in China. Joachim discovered that designers were especially forthcoming about their concerns and problems with demanding, abusive, and insecure clients during smoke breaks — where they huddled together outside the office in small groups. Joachim had never smoked in his life (and still doesn't), but he learned how to smoke just so he could fit in.

While it wasn't the focus of Joachim's research, he heard constant complaints, suggestions, and jokes about assholes during smoke breaks and other "backstage" times and places. Joachim described an especially vile client to me who treated designers as "essentially his own servants to do as he pleased with at any given moment" and who demanded immediate responses to any call or email from the project manager "regardless of the actual severity or immediacy of the problem." Joachim observed, "To deal with this onslaught, during breaks, if a message came in from that client, the project manager would announce it to the team. Then they'd place bets on whether she would also get a call or text before lunch, the coffee run, or the current smoke break was over. It was like you could never truly escape, and only some dark humor during a brief break provided some relief and symbolic resistance to help them to continue without hating the situation too much."

Finally, sociologist Spencer Cahill at the University of South Florida led a fascinating — and creepy — study of bathrooms as backstage areas. Cahill and five research assistants spent over a hundred hours observing behavior in public bathrooms at shopping malls, universities, bars, and restaurants. Beyond the obvious biological needs served by bathrooms, Cahill and his students found that bathrooms provided temporary shelter from upsetting people and situations. As they put it, "once the door to the stall is closed, it is transformed into the occupying individual's private, albeit temporary, retreat from the demands of public life."

In addition to being a place where people can "keep one's personal front in a state of good repair," bathrooms provide a sanctuary for people who feel hurt by jerks to recover and compose themselves. The Western cultural stereotype is that bathrooms provide a place where women can go to cry. Cahill provides an illustration from a Margaret Atwood novel about a woman who was sitting at a bar with friends and realized she was crying — so she locked herself "into one of the plushy-pink cubicles and wept for several minutes." Cahill also describes how, especially for women, bathrooms are a place for collective escape and recovery.

And it isn't just women who flee to the bathroom to compose themselves. In 2009, Goldman Sachs' CEO Lloyd Blankfein told the *New York Times* that, early in his career, the group he led had lost a lot of money. So he went to his boss to propose a solution. Blankfein's boss said the solution was fine and then gave Blankfein some unexpected advice:

> *I turned to walk out of the room, and he said: "Lloyd, just one second before you go. Why don't you stop in the men's room first and throw some water on your face, because if people see you looking as green as you look, they'll jump out the window."*

The survival lesson from studies and stories on backstage regions is that, to reduce your exposure and to recharge your defenses, it helps to find — and if necessary, invent — asshole-free zones where you and others can take temporary refuge.

EARLY WARNING SYSTEMS

People who do a lot of asshole wrangling often band together to prepare for and dodge incoming jerks. Readers including assembly workers, engineers, U.S. Army officers, and priests have explained to me how — when known assholes are inbound — texts, emails, and whispers start flying so people can prepare to hide, leave, or assume a safe pose until the threat passes. Other groups develop methods for spreading information about whether clients, superstars, or bosses are in good or bad moods. In some places, the boss's administrative assistant is recruited to inform colleagues when the boss is in a foul mood (and should be avoided or handled with care) or feeling upbeat (and it is a good time to visit or raise a sensitive subject).

Consider Jonathan Orenstein, the volatile CEO of Mesa Airlines, who the *New York Times* profiled in a 2007 story with the headline "Approach Boss with Caution." The *Times* described Orenstein as "loud, volatile, insulting, doesn't listen to the other perspective." Stacy Heath, his former assistant, estimated he was in a bad mood 60% of the time. As Orenstein's assistant, "her tasks included tracking his mood and warning executives away from a meeting with the boss." After Heath was promoted to a management role, she started calling Orenstein's new assistant for the same reason: "They would call and say, 'Is he in a good mood?' I used to laugh, but I do it now, too."

Or take the alert issued in *The Proposal,* a 2009 film where Sandra Bullock plays a cruel and calculating New York book editor. As she approaches the office, her executive assistant (played by Ryan Reynolds) emails his colleagues "THE WITCH IS ON HER BROOM." In an instant, the gossiping, eating, and screwing around stops, people scurry back to their cubicles, and each pretends to do something that looks productive.

You can also develop your own warning systems for demeaning clients and customers. My favorite came in an email from a former crossing guard who worked at an international border of the old Soviet Union. When he or his colleagues encountered an abusive traveler at the first or "primary" inspection point, they marked the paperwork like this:

He explained, "This insured that the level of subsequent inspection corresponded to the indicators of a-holity demonstrated at the primary check point. Of course, if questioned why this diagram was on the form, the explanation was that the person was a target for inspection."

With the rise of social media, warning systems have become more sophisticated. OpenTable, a popular Internet restaurant reservation service in the United States, not only enables customers to write reviews; restaurant employees can also add notes about customers, which — among other purposes — warns colleagues at their restaurant about incoming assholes. That's what happens at Danny Meyer's Union Square Hospitality Group, which includes such fancy restaurants as Union Square Cafe, Gramercy Tavern, Blue Smoke, Jazz Standard, The Modern, Maialino, Untitled, North End Grill, and Marta. In August 2012, the website *Grub Street* reported that Danny Meyer's staff makes extensive use of "codes and notes on what kind of customer they really are" on OpenTable. For example, a "customer with an S.O.E. note means they have a 'sense of entitlement.'" An insider from Danny Meyer's operation told *Grub Street* that the company is an "empire of niceness" and dedicated to accommodating every customer, but "if you're an asshole to us, it gets written down and you're treated accordingly." In September of 2012, the *New York Times* piece "What Restaurants Know (About You)" added that at many restaurants that use OpenTable, "customers with bad reputations are often flagged HWC, handle with care. And if there's an 86 on your profile, chances are you will be making alternative plans for dinner."

MIX, MATCH, AND IMPROVISE

Each avoidance technique can help people limit their exposure to others who treat them like dirt, and in turn, diminish the damage and risk of "catching" and spreading such ugliness. Check out the handy summary of these "contamination and contagion busters" at the end of the chapter. The methods here, however, provide relief and protection in wildly varied ways — and for most asshole problems, a few of the techniques will work and the rest won't. I wish I could devise a complete survival checklist that works for every asshole problem — something like airplane pilots use before every takeoff. Alas, jerks do their dirty work in so many ways and so many places that every asshole problem requires a custom strategy. It's on you to craft a blend of tactics that is right given the nuances and quirks of your predicament; your strengths, weaknesses, and goals; and how you want to feel about yourself when you look back later on.

Consider an inspired solution that one CEO devised for reducing her exposure to a flaming "boardhole" and seizing a modicum of control over his incoming invective. When she was CEO of a small software firm, she had a board member who screamed and swore at her whenever they spoke. He was so abusive that the CEO did everything she could to avoid face-to-face meetings with him. Instead, as I told *Forbes,* she scheduled regular phone calls with him, where "she put the phone on mute and did her nails," turned the volume of his voice way down, and checked back "every three to four minutes to see if he was still yelling." After a while, the boardhole would have spewed out most of his venom, calmed down a bit, and she could have something resembling a civil and constructive conversation.

In her story, you see hints of the avoidance strategies I've discussed — distancing and dodging. I love her use of the mute and sound volume buttons (which is even better than walking out of a bad meeting) and how the technology — the phone — helped her engage with a "lower resolution" version of the boardhole — she was spared his angry sneer, red face, and the disgusting veins popping out on his forehead. And when she took her shoes off, put her feet on her desk, and did her toenails, the ritual soothed her and turned her attention elsewhere. The combination of the mute button and doing her nails not only reduced the duration and intensity of abuse;

this blend also helped her to become emotionally detached from the ugly situation. I dig more into the virtues of emotional detachment and other "mind tricks that protect your soul" from assholes in the next chapter.

For now, let's focus on the big lesson illustrated by that CEO. This book provides key ingredients that you can use to create a survival strategy that works best *for you*. I also offer studies, solutions, and stories because, if you feel besieged by assholes, they show that you are not alone, that there are protective steps you can take, and — for most people — life gets much better. It's up to you, and perhaps those who can help you, to develop, experiment with, and keep tweaking your own survival strategy given the particular weirdness you face — just like that clever CEO did when she scheduled phone calls instead of face-to-face meetings, hit the mute button, and painted her nails.

ASSHOLE AVOIDANCE TIPS
Contamination and Contagion Busters

1. **Ride the Allen curve.** Can you entice the local assholes to move just a little farther away from you? As MIT's Tom Allen showed, even an extra ten feet can help. And if you can somehow get them to move to new digs, in another building or on a different floor, it is almost as good as shipping them to another country.
2. **So close but so far.** If you must go to gatherings or are forced to be in close proximity to jerks, can you sit or stand even just a few extra feet away? Try to choose a place where it's difficult to make eye contact with your tormentor, such as on the

same side of the table but as far away from him or her as possible.

3. **Dodge and duck out.** Can you avoid encounters with people who nauseate you and unleash your inner devil? Can you figure out how to be home or on the road when they are around — or arrive late or leave early for meetings, collaborative work, or social gatherings that you can't skip?

4. **The rhythm method.** Are you locked in a relationship with one of those assholes who takes pleasure every time you react with obvious unhappiness? If so, can you slow the rhythm? Try to delay and deny your tormentor reinforcement by waiting as long as you can before you respond to nasty messages and phone calls. And meet with him or her as rarely as you can.

5. **An invisibility cloak.** Are you stuck in an asshole-rich setting, where powerful superiors, clients, or citizens treat you as if you were invisible — except when you commit some real or imagined crime, and then they dump all over you? Perhaps that invisibility can provide you with protective camouflage. You might blend into the background by saying as little as possible, being boring, doing work that is neither terrible nor terrific, and hiding behind a bland and blank expression.

6. **Bully blockers.** Can you find a boss who shields you from the assholes — or perhaps gently train him or her to do it? Or can you find or recruit a flak catcher, someone who wrangles with rude and overbearing customers, employees, users, or citizens so that you don't have to?

7. **Tag-team partners.** Can you develop a formal or informal rotation system so that everyone gets about the same amount of exposure to known jerks or tasks that are more asshole-in-

tensive? That way, everybody gets the fair share of abuse (and relief).

8. **Go backstage for temporary relief.** Find and use a "safety zone" where assholes aren't allowed to go or can't find you, where you have time to recover from the latest insults to your soul and prepare for the next, and can commiserate with and support fellow targets. It might be a dedicated place like a teachers' lounge, or the local Starbucks or watering hole, or it could be just a quiet hallway or a nearby park.

9. **Activate the early warning system.** Work with your colleagues and comrades to warn each other of incoming assholes — so you can hide from them, be on your best behavior, steer them away from people and places that will trigger their disdain or rage, and perhaps prepare to screw your tormentor over. A sign on the door that says "The asshole is in" probably will get you in trouble; but discreet use of phone calls, messages, emails, or social media just might do the trick.

5   Mind Tricks That Protect Your Soul

REMEMBER HOW, back in chapter 2, West Point "plebe" Becky Margiotta twisted her thoughts to survive the nonstop hazing? Let's dig a bit deeper into how she reduced the sting.

One day, early in that first year, Becky triggered a storm of ridicule from several upper-class cadets after she failed to repeat every story on the front page of the day's *New York Times* (a common "mistake"). They stood "two inches from my nose and screamed at me" about all the ways she was a failure as a person and professional. Becky had an epiphany that day; rather than taking this abuse personally, she started thinking of these in-your-face antics as "incredibly entertaining." She stopped worrying that the game was rigged, that she was destined to provoke constant humiliation, and that she was at risk of losing composure and thus the mandated "military bearing."

Instead, she focused on how imaginative and funny the upper-class cadets were as they hazed plebes. Becky became so impressed with their "wit and skill," so to speak, that when it was directed at her, it rattled her far less. At times, Becky found their insults, taunts, and petty punishments so hilarious that she couldn't suppress her laughter, which got her into more trouble (they screamed things like "What is so funny?" and "This is no laughing matter!"), which just made it all seem even more amusing.

Becky dealt with assholes by *reframing* their behavior so it was less upsetting and less threatening to her—that's how therapists who practice cognitive behavioral therapy (and many researchers) would put it. Cognitive behavioral therapy is the most widely used evidence-based approach for treating mental health problems. It's grounded in the idea that dysfunctional thinking can shape a patient's mood and behavior in destructive ways. As University of Pennsylvania's Judith Beck explains, such therapy helps patients to see their experiences in a different and more positive light—which enables them to feel better and to engage in more constructive behaviors. Part of the therapy entails nudging patients to reframe difficulties and concerns as being less upsetting, or even as good things. Social psychologists and other researchers have shown that reframing (or "reappraising") disturbing facts or distressing experiences in a more positive light—while not a cure-all—can provide relief. For example, whether the same experience is portrayed as a fun and exciting challenge—versus a distressing threat—can transform how people feel and perform in response.

Adam Alter from New York University and his colleagues did remarkable research on such reframing with elementary school kids in North Carolina and with undergraduates at Princeton University. They found that African American students in both groups performed considerably better on a math test when it was framed as a challenging questionnaire (i.e., as interesting or intellectually provocative) rather than as a threatening test (that would show how smart they were "right now" or assess their basic ability). It was the same test, but *seeing it* as a challenge boosted their confidence and turned their attention away from negative cultural stereotypes about African Americans and their allegedly disadvantaged educational backgrounds (when such stereotypes are made vivid to African

American students, studies show that their learning, self-confidence, and performance suffer).

Reframing is a common defense against workplace assholes. Dana Yagil and her colleagues at the University of Haifa surveyed 225 Israeli employees about how they dealt with supervisors who abused them via ridicule, bad-mouthing, embarrassment, the silent treatment, and other cruel words and deeds. They measured reframing by asking if employees told themselves things such as "this is only a job" and "this is a small, unimportant matter." Yagil's team found that reframing was among the main tactics that abused employees turned to for emotional shelter.

Similarly, a study in a Spanish telecommunications company found that bullied employees who engaged in "psychological detachment" by actively thinking about more pleasant things and "switching off" during nonwork hours suffered less emotional strain (e.g., unhappiness, depression, lost sleep). Detached employees were also less obsessed with exacting revenge — they thought less about getting even with bosses and coworkers who humiliated, ridiculed, and spread nasty rumors about them.

This chapter unpacks reframing strategies and related "mind tricks" that can provide protection even when you can't or won't escape, reduce your exposure, or fight the jerks who bug and badger you. Changing how you construe people and events can be like putting on a protective flak jacket that shields you from incoming assholes. Most of these tricks work best when you join forces with friends, coaches, bosses, coworkers, or fellow targets to develop "frames" that work for you and others in the same boat. These tricks still help when you go it alone. But when you build such interpretations with others who you can trust, they can verify that you aren't crazy and that you really are under siege. And you have allies to help you get through tough times when the brutes and backstabbers are on the warpath or your self-confidence wavers — and you can help them get through rough times in return.

The power of reframing — and having others to help you with it — pervades the advice that an employee assistance counselor at a U.S. government facility gives to the bullied employees he serves. This counselor wrote me that his job was "to get folks to survive in Assholeville" and outlined the three key steps he follows:

1. He advises the abused employee to "take a survey," to talk to fellow employees to make sure that the "managing asshole" is not singling him or her out for abuse. These conversations with colleagues are crucial because, if the manager is treating the employee about as badly as everyone else, then the employee can stop "indicting" him or herself "for creating a bad situation."

2. If the offending manager is, in fact, an equal opportunity asshole, the counselor asks of the aggrieved: "Why are you depressed and anxious when he does act as you define him?" And "Why stress about an asshole doing asshole stuff?"

3. If the employee is certain that "yes, this is an asshole," the counselor encourages detachment — one of the reframing strategies I've already mentioned and will talk about more. One of his favorite detachment strategies is to encourage employees to think of themselves as a spectator or observer — not as a player — in a competition where the goal is to predict their tormentor's next move. He explained, "The

employee takes control of their experience by looking at the facts and predicting outcomes. My clients are often delighted when they are able to report, 'I guessed he would do that and he did. What an asshole!'"

Each of these steps entails helping depressed and anxious employees to change their definition of the situation — *not* the situation itself. In addition, employees trust their new definition because it is formed and sustained through multiple conversations with the counselor and fellow targets. It helps when people turn to each other for support and find that they aren't alone or defective. They learn that their peers are dealing with or have survived asshole problems, which gives them hope and confidence that they can too.

Now let's dig into some specific mind tricks that can protect your soul.

You aren't to blame.   Employees at that U.S. government facility suffered less after convincing themselves that they weren't to blame for their tormentor's behavior. As that counselor suggested, they had no reason to berate themselves because "Why stress about an asshole doing asshole stuff?" Cognitive behavioral therapists describe this as reversing or dampening destructive "personalization" where "you believe others are behaving negatively because of you, without first considering more plausible interpretations for their behavior."

Experiments at Stanford University by Jens Blechert and his colleagues confirm the protective power of such reframing (they called it "reappraisal"). When they showed Stanford students pictures of angry people and then gave them a few minutes of reappraisal training (e.g., "Imagine this person is not angry at you but just had a bad day or a fight with his boss"), then seeing additional pictures of angry people no longer upset them (as the pictures had the first time). In contrast, students who weren't taught such "it's not my fault" reappraisals continued to get upset by viewing pictures of angry people. Jens Blechert's talents as both a therapist and researcher are evident in his 2011 interview in *HealthDay News* about the implications of this coping study. Blechert concluded that "if you're trained with reappraisal, and you know your boss is frequently in a bad mood, you can prepare yourself to go into a meeting," and when your boss does "scream and yell and shout," your negative reactions will be weaker and, in fact, you may have none at all.

Prison guards use a similar tactic to take the sting out of inmates' insults and threats. Two researchers I've already mentioned, Katy DeCelles (who advised "don't engage with crazy") and Michel Anteby (who studied TSA employees with Curtis Chan), teamed up to study the emotional responses of correctional officers who worked in U.S. state prisons. Their interviews with, and observations of, 113 correctional officers revealed that "not taking it personally" was a key mind trick that officers used to dampen their negative reactions to inmates, see them as humans rather than as caged animals, and set the stage for treating them in caring rather than cruel or apathetic ways.

DeCelles and Anteby found "this shielding behavior was especially prevalent when it came to disrespect, insults, and threats directed towards officers." An officer told them, "Well, I have tried not to look at things as a personal assault on me," and he tried to "step back" and construe prisoners' insults and anger as if they were not attacking him. Instead, he framed their outbursts as an affront to the authority figure they "see on a daily basis, day in, day out," not toward him as a person who provoked their anger or deserved to be blamed for their plight.

Finally, a warning about this "depersonalization" or "it's not my fault" defense: As I show in chapter 7, many people who fuel asshole problems, or who *are* the problem, still blame others. Sure, even if you are an asshole, convincing yourself that you really are a swell person may protect your mental health. Such a denial can, however, come back to bite you. Your bad behavior may attract and breed fellow assholes, who then turn their fire on you (being a jerk yourself doesn't necessarily protect you from fellow jerks). And, as I warned in *The No Asshole Rule,* treating others like dirt is also risky because you create enemies — who wait for just the right occasion for payback. In many social networks and organizations, Groucho Marx's old line "time wounds all heels" is prophetic.

Downplay the threat.   This "it's not that bad" tactic entails first acknowledging you are in Jerkworld, but construing the meanies as less evil or harmful than you once did. This was part of Becky Margiotta's strategy at West Point; by seeing the hazing by upper-class cadets as "hilarious," she rendered their haranguing and punishments as less threatening in her mind.

Skilled therapists and leaders do something similar to help clients and followers identify destructive thoughts that are untrue or exaggerated in their minds — to help them view their situation in a more positive (or at least less negative) light. In cognitive behavioral therapy, therapists work with patients to change their thinking when they have "tunnel vision" or use "mental filters" that cause them to fixate on the negative parts of a situation. And they help patients to question and then change destructive and seemingly permanent labels that they apply to themselves or to others despite "evidence that might more reasonably lead to a less disastrous conclusion."

If you are dealing with assholes, or helping others do so, such reframing can provide protection. When I conducted the study of telephone bill collectors described in chapter 4, I learned that collectors often said things like "that was nothing, I've had a lot worse" to reduce the distress they or colleagues felt from ugly encounters with debtors. After my classroom training, I spent several days where I watched and listened, and then made my own calls, under the guidance of an experienced collector. During one call, I was rattled by a curt debtor who complained that I had called during dinner, took too long to make my point, and he had missed just one payment and my harassment was over the top. After the call, the experienced collector helped me reframe the experience, explaining that after I did more calls, I would realize the debtor I had spoken to hadn't insulted, yelled, or swore at me, and that it was good he sounded annoyed because it meant that he was upset enough to pay (but not so upset to refuse to pay out of spite). He said it was about as good as a call gets — the debtor answered the phone, wasn't obnoxious, and paid the bill.

I later saw that experienced collectors often responded to angry, dishonest, or clueless debtors by telling colleagues that it was no big deal and recounting war stories about debtors who were far more crazy or cruel. Those war stories not only helped comfort and calm fellow collectors; telling such tales also created "social glue" that bonded collectors together, provided entertainment and gave them a chance to laugh at debtors and themselves, spread tricks of the trade, and gave collectors a chance to brag.

Consider a manager at a city-planning department who did layoffs during a budget crisis — which triggered an ugly bout of asshole poisoning, especially by several disgruntled staff members who kept "lobbing" angry, insulting, and false comments at and about management. This troubled manager recruited a veteran government leader to do what was, in essence, a reframing intervention for the department. The leader had one-on-one conversations with individuals and then gathered them all for a meeting. He started off by saying, "Let's get one thing straight. I've met them and your managers aren't half as bad as you think they are, nor half as good as they think they are." The leader added that, he knew from experience, "there will be one or two of you sitting near the back of the room with your hands across your chests, just waiting to hurl rocks no matter what we are talking about."

The besieged manager explained how this reframing cut two ways — it conveyed to the staff that their managers weren't so bad, and to managers that the staff wasn't so bad, that people on both sides were exaggerating the threat. This example also demonstrates how reframing can change behavior — not just the definition of a situation. The manager wrote that the leader's reframing not only enabled everyone in the room to feel less threatened, it "stigmatized bad stuff on both sides and allowed us to laugh and talk more easily."

Focus on the silver lining. This mind trick entails admitting to yourself that your treatment sucks, but focusing on the upside — on the good you are reaping from the asshole. It's a variation of the "it's not really that bad" reframe.

It can be useful for getting through encounters or extended relationships with nasty people, or for helping you feel better when you look back at it all later. For example, journalist Andrew Beaujon wrote a charming, and rather disturbing, piece for the Poynter Institute's website in 2014 that asked, "Why Do Journalists Remember Nasty Editors Fondly?" He put the question to his colleague Jill

Geisler. In addition to noting the pride that some journalists felt about surviving what was akin to fraternity and sorority hazing from a tough and demanding editor, she pointed to a pair of silver linings.

First, survivors emphasized the crucial lessons that they learned about journalism from these bossholes. In Geisler's words, "In fact, there WAS a pony under all that poop. The pony was smart and taught them some skills that made them better. That's why the managers got 'idiosyncrasy credits' for the other boorish (but not dishonest) behaviors." The second upside was that nasty editors sometimes threw a few crumbs of confidence to the young journalist; that small island of praise in a sea of cruelty felt mighty good. As Geisler explained, "When the meanest SOB in the valley tells you, 'Kid, if you get your head out of your butt you might actually make it in this business,' some kids feel special — and they cling to that."

Rise above it.   Former U.S. First Lady Michelle Obama used this reframing strategy in her speech at the 2016 Democratic National Convention in Philadelphia. Mrs. Obama described how she and President Obama talked to their teenage daughters Malia and Sasha about the "hateful language they hear from public figures on TV." She said, "We explain that when someone is cruel or acts like a bully, you don't stoop to their level. No, our motto is: when they go low, we go high."

Much as the former First Lady and her husband did to protect their family from the relentless insults and accusations that every U.S. president faces, this mind trick entails telling yourself and those you care about to stick to the high road and refuse to stoop to your tormentor's level — and that doing so will mean you are a better human being than those lowlifes. Not only does this strategy help targets take pride in their superiority; by responding to the malice with a sense of calm, civility, and even warmth, there is less chance of getting into a shit fight — of triggering a vicious circle of mutual hostility.

This isn't just a strategy that politicians and their families can use (and one I wish more would use). It's at the heart of how baristas at Philz Coffee are trained, frame, and treat their customers. Philz is a chain of thirty-five stores headquartered in San Francisco. When I talked to CEO Jacob Jaber, he said Philz is dedicated to treating customers with warmth, to "crafting a perfect cup to every individual customer's taste," which — between the experience and great coffee — results in "cups of love." Jacob insists that baristas be nice even to rude customers. He explained, sometimes, customers realize that they've been jerks and turn nicer. They even apologize now and then. Regardless, being nice to nasty customers is a source of pride for Philz's baristas — for being able to resist the temptation to stoop to the jerk's level and return the "bad vibe." As Jacob put it, when customers are assholes, he just tells baristas, "Be nice to 'em. Fuck 'em. But be nice."

After talking with Jacob, I wanted to learn his employees' perspective on nasty customers; after all, just because a CEO says something doesn't mean it reflects how the people on the front lines act and feel. I recruited Deanna Badizadegan (my former student and research assistant) to interview several baristas, a shift manager, and a store manager. Deanna met them at two Philz locations in San Francisco; each served diverse customers including young tech workers, bankers and lawyers, homeless people, tourists, college students, and teenagers.

Deanna was struck by how vehement each Philz employee was that "the job is all about 'bettering people's days' — it doesn't matter how shitty of a person they are." The Philz employees had numerous stories about offensive customers — control freaks ("they don't even want the coffee; they just want to have their little 'I'm in charge' fix for the morning"), neurotic/OCD types (who want "a super specific cup"), and worst of all, the classist ones ("the person who thinks he's better than you" because they have more money or a fancy job). Each employee repeated the mantra that they lived and pressed their Philz coworkers to use as protective armor against nasty customers: "Kill 'em with kindness."

As Jacob Jaber implied, his employees took great pride in sticking to the high road and viewed losing their cool as unprofessional. They were also proud about stepping in to save beleaguered fellow baristas who were on the verge of losing their composure and of how their relentless kindness sometimes "flips" nasty customers ("who eventually warm up to you"). A shift leader summed up this collective devotion to taking the high road like this: "Why should I be mad at someone for demanding a perfect cup of coffee? If I can't do that, maybe I shouldn't work here — it's all about the mind-set!"

Develop sympathy for the devil.   Even if a jerk doesn't deserve to be excused or let off easy, this approach can help you feel less demeaned and de-energized. It helped me deal with a colleague who cares deeply about his students and who enables them to achieve wonderful things, but is otherwise unpleasant, temperamental, and selfish. He has hollered at, insulted, and threatened dozens of other professors and staff members (usually over trivial matters), resists sharing resources or ideas, demands more space and money than others with similar needs, and — unless he wants something from them — treats most people that he encounters every day as if they were invisible.

I don't work with him directly. Yet, at one point, his antics were getting on my nerves. One year, he taught after me in the same classroom. While my class was in session, he often pressured me to dismiss it early so he could then set up for his class. He also hollered at several people I admire. I found myself spending several hours each week being pissed off at him, even though I couldn't stop his antics (well, I tried and failed, perhaps I should have tried harder) and I had limited contact with him.

Then I began using a mind trick that eliminated nearly all my anger toward and rumination about this petulant professor. I thought of all the ways his life had been difficult and all the good that he has done. I said to myself things like "He is like a porcupine with a heart of gold" or, to steal a line from a Google engineer, "He is a guy with a bad user interface but a good operating system." By developing sympathy for this devil, and allowing myself to forgive him, I've altered my perceptions so that he stopped driving me nuts.

This kind of reframing strategy is bolstered by theory and research on forgiveness. It shows that, even when a jerk doesn't apologize, and you don't express forgiveness to them, forgiving him or her in your heart can help you let go of the hurt — and you should do so without condoning, downplaying, or forgetting the offense. Research on bullying and "interpersonal transgressions" such as lies, insults, and broken promises shows that forgiveness helps victims to let go of their simmering resentment and thoughts of evening the score.

In an experiment by psychologist Charlotte van Oyen Witvliet and her colleagues, college students were asked to think of someone who mistreated, offended, or hurt them. As the experiment unfolded, students were prompted to alternate between unforgiving thoughts that involved staying angry and "harboring the grudge" versus forgiving thoughts that entailed "empathizing with the offender" and "granting forgiveness." Forgiving thoughts reduced students' feelings of anger and sadness, increased their sense of being in control, and also reduced physiological signs of distress, including elevated heart rate and blood pressure. Unforgiving thoughts had the opposite effects. This study dovetails with research on bullied schoolchildren that found victims who forgive cruel classmates are plagued by less social anxiety and fewer thoughts of revenge, and also report greater self-esteem.

The upshot is that even if your tormentors don't deserve to be let off the hook, pardoning them for their sins can free you from being haunted by them and will bolster feelings that you are master of your own fate.

Focus on the funny side.   Humor, jokes, and laughter have a dark side. Canadian researcher Rod Martin devoted over thirty years to studying humor and laughter. As Martin shows in *The Psychology of Humor,* when insults or threats are coated in humor or sarcasm, they sting just as hard, or ever harder, and yet they are sometimes more socially acceptable.

"Relax, it's just a joke" is a standard defense that assholes use to justify their terrible words and deeds. Yet humor is both a weapon *and* a shield. Framing the cruelty or insensitivity that they aim at you as funny, absurd, or ridiculous can dampen the damage. Research that uses Martin's "Coping Humor Scale" shows that people in distressing situations suffer less emotional and physical harm when they see the humor in it all. These are people who agree with statements such as, "I have often found that my problems have been greatly reduced when I tried to find something funny in them" and "I can usually find something to laugh or joke about even in trying situations." Perhaps this is why Annie Hogh and Andrea Dofradottir found that Danish employees who experienced frequent (even daily) slander and nasty teasing turned to humor as a coping strategy considerably more than those employees who experienced occasional bullying or none at all. It seems that finding and focusing on the funny side and absurdity of an asshole's moves — and how you and others respond — can serve as protective armor.

We've seen the protective powers of humor throughout this book. The targets quoted here often anoint nasty people with funny nicknames including "boardhole," "bosshole," "Darth Vader," "the idea man," "not a mentor but a *torr-mentor*," "A$$hole Factory," "grinfucker," and "the Sea Witch." Humor helps reduce the pain for my Stanford colleagues and me too. As I was writing this chapter, I had what started as a somber conversation with a Stanford staff member about her overly controlling boss. Soon, we were both laughing about an episode straight out of the TV show *The Office* or the cult-classic film *Office Space*. This micromanager had taken to timing how long one of her underlings spent in the bathroom and, when she returned, peppering her subordinate with questions like "Do you really need to spend so much time putting on your makeup?" We knew this boss had embarrassed the targeted staff member and struck fear in the hearts of peers who observed and heard of these antics — and we had sympathy for their plight. But seeing the sheer ridiculousness of it all, and sharing a laugh, turned something that was upsetting to both of us into a source of entertainment, which made it hurt less and enabled both of us to feel less helpless — at least we could change how we felt about it, even if we couldn't stop such nonsense.

Look back from the future.   The mantra here is: "This too shall pass." When you hit a rough patch, tell yourself that it's temporary. Think about all the other upsetting people and problems you've faced in the past, and how when you look back at them now, they don't bother you, it was no big deal, or it was even for the best. Researchers Emma Bruehlman-Senecal and Ozlem Ayduk at the University of California have documented the stress-reducing powers of "temporal distancing." As they put it, "Humans have a unique capacity for mental time travel. We can transcend the here-and-now by both envisioning the past and imagining the future."

This duo conducted six studies that show that when people face stressors both large and small (from ending a long-term relationship to doing poorly on an exam), if they focus on how they will feel in the distant future (rather than the near future), they feel less immediate worry, fear, anxiety, anger, sadness, disappointment, and guilt. Such people are prone to agree with statements like "I don't think I'll be upset anymore in one week" and "I focused on how the current consequences of the problem will fade over time."

There seem to be two reasons why temporal distancing helps people cope with a current stress. First, most people are more optimistic about the future than the present. So they expect that things in their lives will be better down the road, including what is upsetting them right now. Second, and especially crucial, is the protective power of perceived impermanence. By looking to the distant future, people are comforted when they realize that their current troubles and the associated emotional distress are just temporary — they remember that clichés such as "this too shall pass," "time heals all wounds," and "humor is tragedy plus time" are often true.

To deal with the assholes you encounter right now, imagine it is a few hours, days, months, or years later (depending on how long you expect the abuse to last), and focus on how much less upset you will be about it then. So there is no need to be so preoccupied and upset right now. That's what a former Costco cashier who wrote me did to survive her terrible boss. Her supervisor criticized her, glared at her, and swore under his breath at her—and gave her only one compliment in six months. She focused her thoughts on how, by the time she got home that night, the day's events would all seem like no big deal. And, after she quit, that it would be nothing, just something she had to endure to move to a better place. Such time shifting helped her get through many tough days—and to move on to a higher-paying job with a much better boss.

Use emotional detachment.   This is the "frankly, asshole, I don't give a damn" strategy. Yes, it can have big downsides, including losing your job. The most valuable and admirable people care deeply about and give everything they've got to help their colleagues, fellow volunteers, customers, clients, and such. Evidence from researchers at Gallup and many other investigators shows that when employees are more "engaged" in their work and committed to their bosses and colleagues, they are more productive, cooperative, happy, creative, prone to put in extra effort, and less likely to quit; conversely, disengagement has the opposite effects and plagues many organizations and teams. And consider a rather horrifying study of burned-out nurses conducted on 161 Pennsylvania hospitals: "cognitively detached" nurses washed their hands less often and less well, which was linked to a spike in urinary tract and "surgical site" infections among patients.

The lesson is that emotional disengagement, detachment, or distancing (or whatever you prefer to call it) is a sometimes terrible and entirely predictable human response to bad situations. When people treat you like dirt, it's difficult to give them your full attention and total effort. For better or worse, this reframing strategy packs a wallop. Practicing the fine art of not giving a shit about people who mistreat you — honing your ability to tune them out — can save your sanity, shield your physical health, and keep you from hurting the people you love.

The discussion of emotional detachment in *The No Asshole Rule* sparked hundreds of emails and conversations with readers about when and how to use this mind trick. I've also tracked research on psychological detachment, distancing, and related coping methods over the years. I view detachment as a method that everybody ought to use to cope with assholes (and other stressors too), as a powerful anesthetic that helps people endure and recover from scorn, contempt, and other insults to their souls. And over the years, I've developed a more nuanced view of detachment, which is a rough hierarchy of increasing intensity. The essence is that even people who deal with mild asshole problems can benefit from some detachment, and as abuse becomes more severe and pervasive, more intense detachment is justified and necessary. Here's my hierarchy.

Level 1: Tune out during downtime.   This is the lowest level of detachment — the assholes at work might be driving you crazy, but when you aren't working, it helps to turn your attention and effort elsewhere so you can recover your equilibrium, enjoy life, and marshal resources for the rough times ahead. We've already seen that when besieged employees ruminate too much about their horrible bosses, coworkers, or customers, it is a symptom of a severe asshole problem and that they are coping with it badly. Recall the marketing manager in chapter 2 who worked at the "A$$hole Factory" for seven years. He suffered so much, in part, because he was unable to detach from his job when he was off work. He said, "I would come home from work and lose my temper with my partner for no reason."

At least a dozen studies have used a measure of psychological detachment developed by Sabine Sonnentag and Charlotte Fritz to examine the impact of "switching off" or mentally disengaging from work during off hours. Most of these studies have found that employees were better off when they could avoid repetitive thoughts, worries, and ruminations about what happened and will happen at work. They had fewer physical and mental health problems, fewer sleep problems, less fatigue, better job performance and productivity, and less conflict between work and family roles.

The challenge, of course, is *how* to detach from work. Since the advent of smartphones, many of us are "always on." This is an obstacle that bosses, coworkers, friends, relatives, and partners can help each other overcome. Try to resist your cell phone addiction. Put away your phone and turn off your work email whenever you can. And ask your colleagues, friends, and lovers to nudge you when you slip. Or try the trick that Padmasree Warrior uses. This veteran technology executive is currently U.S. CEO of NextEV, an electric car company; *Fortune* called her the "Queen of the Electric Car Biz." According to TechRepublic's website, at the end of every day, Warrior takes twenty minutes, "finds a quiet space wherever she may be, turns off all her electronics, and meditates."

Unless it is essential, try to avoid sending work emails at night or on weekends. And, if you can't help yourself, at least do what my wife Marina does; she is the CEO of the Girl Scouts of Northern California, which employs about 150 people and serves some 44,000 girls and 31,000 adult volunteers. Marina does sometimes work nights and weekends; she must to keep up with this demanding job. But she doesn't want her staff to get the message that they should work such long hours too. So when she writes emails on nights and weekends, unless it's urgent, she waits to send them during regular work hours.

No matter where you work, it helps to develop little rituals that say to yourself and to others, "I am off" and to create clear separation between work (or other demanding roles) and the rest of your life. Along these lines, Katy DeCelles did another study of correctional officers (this time with colleague Chen-Bo Zhong) on dealing with work that is viewed as emotionally and physically "dirty." Katy and Chen-Bo found that making a clear-cut and conscious emotional separation between being on and off duty helped officers cope with the insults, anger, humiliation, and physical filth that came with their jobs. As an officer who practiced such mental separation put it, "I am not going to take my job home with me, and I think that's the only reason why I am so sane after eleven and a half years." Officers used diverse rituals to mark an overt and complete transition from work to other roles. One deliberately shut the prison gate behind him as a reminder that he was no longer a correctional officer until he returned to work again. Another told Katy that he left "his work stress on his 'time card'" by 'washing his hands after work,' which helped him to 'not take it home.'"

Level 2: Detach or tune out during just the worst of times. In addition to recovering when you are off work and other down times, this level entails responding to bad experiences and people by giving as little of yourself as you can, just going through the motions, thinking about better things, and generally dealing with bullies and backstabbers in emotionally distant and perfunctory ways. But then, when you have encounters with more civilized people, you "switch on" your caring and compassion and give them your full self and talents.

That's how a special education teacher in Chicago dealt with a colleague's constant critique of her skills, appearance, and squeaky voice: "I stopped listening to him. When he spoke, I would just think about the kids in my class and how I could help them." It's also how a U.S. Air Force Academy cadet who was determined to graduate and fly planes survived fellow cadets who berated and insulted him. He didn't see the humor in hazing like Becky the West Point plebe did. Instead, he said, "When I encountered an asshole, I looked through him and imagined he wasn't even there. I repeated to myself, 'I want to fly.'" Similarly, a study of Australian nurses in kidney dialysis units found that "emotional distancing" was their main coping strategy — especially to deal with aggressive and insulting patients and fellow nurses who treated them with disdain and disrespect. One nurse told the researchers, "I block, I just think . . . I'm a machine, I'm going to do what I have to do."

There is related evidence that employees protect themselves from dysfunctional conflict themselves by "flattening" the emotions that they feel and express. A study of 459 employees by Ashley Nixon and her colleagues found that people dealt with arguments and disagreements at work by "modifying their visible response to the conflict, through mechanisms such as suppressing negative emotions or expressing fake positive emotions." Similarly, numerous readers reported that when they face demeaning or rude people, they respond to the incoming anger or disrespect with the most boring, vague, and perfunctory responses that they can muster. They said it was a way to give as little of themselves as possible to their tormentors. These readers emphasized that giving nothing back — no anger, no juicy details, no sadness or pain, only the most boring and superficial version of themselves possible — provides assholes less fuel for further hostility, while at the same time is a passive-aggressive form of revenge because it frustrates and bores many meanies.

A government employee wrote me that she was subject to cruel rumors and gossip from several coworkers and blatant "ill will" from two bosses. She developed a host of "non-defensive" responses that helped her survive encounters with the bosses who abused her and ugly interactions with "their confederates." This long list of hollow responses included "Thanks, I will take that into consideration," "I appreciate your input," "I see," "I never looked at it that way," and "I don't have an opinion on that." She explained that such banal comments helped her reveal as little of herself as possible to people who were determined to hurt her, those comments gave them no additional ammunition to use against her, and they were so dull that they helped "dead end" conversations with "the mass of assholes." Alas, this is not how people in healthy relationships communicate with each other—but when people keep insulting and humiliating you, and bad-mouthing and backstabbing you, such vacuous language can create protective emotional distance.

One of my Stanford colleagues adds an inspired twist to this level of detachment. When he has a meeting with one or more people who are prone to be mean, stubborn, or condescending, he distances himself by taking a "clinical" perspective. He pretends that he is like a doctor and his job is to diagnose this intriguing, rare, and extreme case of assholism and to develop the best treatment. When one of his colleagues does something especially offensive, rather than getting angry, he tells himself how lucky he is to see such a "fascinating case" and, much like a physician who is treating a very sick patient, he says to himself things like "That poor devil is in such terrible shape, I feel so bad for him." My creative colleague says that, sometimes, using this "clinical" reframing helps him develop better ways to battle and to calm these difficult characters. But even when it doesn't have any effect on the assholes, the detachment helps keep him unfettered by frustration and anger during rough meetings and to brood about them less after they are over.

Level 3: Tune out as much as you can, most or all of the time.   This is the highest level of detachment, at least short of becoming emotionally distant from everyone and everything in your life (which isn't a healthy response to any situation). It's a strategy that ought to be reserved for those situations where your organization, team, school, or any other place "feels like a prolonged personal insult," where you are constantly treated like dirt, where the abuse comes from every direction, or where there is a relentless downpour of cruel crap from on high.

It entails doing everything you can to give them as little of yourself as possible, to just go through the motions and to tune out as many people as possible, as completely as possible — even if they are right in front of you. Instead, turn your full attention to those people who treat you with respect, to what matters most to you, and to the better days ahead. Your goal is to give the bare minimum of yourself to others, while still protecting yourself from their wrath.

My mother taught me "that anything worth doing is worth doing well." Well, she was wrong. When you are surrounded with vile people, there are things that you still must do to keep your job or to keep the peace, but those jobs aren't worth doing well. An engineer explained to me that his boss, and his boss's boss, and senior management treated his team so badly that they only gave "MVE" (minimum viable effort) — a tactic inspired by best-selling author Eric Ries's MVP concept (minimum viable product). He said, "We decided that those assholes don't deserve any more from us."

Again, extreme detachment has plenty of negative consequences.

As research by Gallup shows, employees who are completely checked out (i.e., working zombies who are the most disengaged) are absent more often, quit at higher rates, are less proud of their company and its products, and are less productive. I am not excusing disengaged employees for their lackluster and sometimes downright lame efforts. But many of their dysfunctional bosses, teams, and organizations are simply reaping what they sow — they've helped create the "working wounded" who struggle day after day to survive some mighty ugly circumstances. And who are wise to save their energy for people who treat them with respect, and perhaps to search for a better job.

THE LIMITS OF REFRAMING

I've summarized the mind tricks in this chapter with the accompanying list to help you play "The Asshole Reframing Game." These are little sayings that can help boost your mental and physical health when you are dealing with vile people and bad behavior — all are grounded in the evidence and practical tips that I covered above.

> **THE ASSHOLE REFRAMING GAME**
>
> **Little Sayings That Can Reduce the Sting**
>
> *You aren't alone . . .*
>
> "A lot of other people are dealing with the same ugly thing. I am not crazy or a bad person."
>
> "We have each other. At least we aren't alone."

You aren't to blame . . .

"I can't take it personally. It's not my fault he acts like such a jerk."

"She is the one who ought to feel terrible. Not me."

Downplay the threat . . .

"Sure she is an asshole, but I've faced much worse."

"The assholes here are wimps compared to other places."

Focus on the silver lining . . .

"There is a pony under that poop."

"We are all getting so much from him that it is worth putting up with his crap."

Rise above it . . .

"I won't stoop to their level. I am better than that."

"When they go low, we go high."

Develop sympathy for the devil . . .

"He is a jerk, but he's been through such hard times that I won't hold it against him."

"I won't forget what she did to me. But I understand why she was so mean even if she was wrong. I forgive her. It's better for me that way."

Focus on the funny side . . .

"It's better to laugh than to cry. And these jerks are actually pretty funny."

Look back from the future . . .

"This too shall pass. Time heals all wounds."

"It will all seem like no big deal when I look back at it later."

Use emotional detachment . . .

Level 1:   "I am just going to do something different and think about something more pleasant tonight."

Level 2:   "When that jerk acts up, I tune her out and imagine she isn't even there" or "I pretend I am a doctor and am diagnosing a fascinating case of assholism, so the more extreme and bizarre, the more intriguing it is."

Level 3:   "I don't care about these terrible people. I am going to give them as little of myself as possible, go through the motions every day, and not let them touch my soul."

Yet relying on only such mind tricks is a dangerous survival strategy. It can fuel the Asshole Blindness that was discussed in chapter 3; reframing alone doesn't change what happens to you or other targets, or the bullies around you; it can change only how you think about your circumstances.

Reframing is a double-edged sword. Several of these little sayings are reminiscent of the "Ten Lies" that I listed in chapter 3 that fuel Asshole Blindness. It can blind you to those situations when escaping from and reducing your exposure to destructive people are far better moves. And it may prevent you from battling bullies and backstabbers that you really can change for the better, defeat, or drive out. In short, reframing alone is an especially suspect strategy when you are confronted with the most abusive and damaging kinds of assholes. Yes, relying on reframing and little else is sometimes necessary for victims trapped in terrible situations, but only as a last resort.

If reframing were a prescription drug rather than a set of coping strategies, I would include a warning label that reads something like "Use with extreme caution in cases of prolonged, extreme, or unlawful abuse including but not limited to sexual harassment, overt or intentional racism, implied or expressed threats of physical harm, sexual assault, and other violent or physically harmful acts. Side effects may include dangerous denial of and no actual reduction in objective abuse."

Now, it's time to talk about fighting back.

6   Fighting Back

MAKE NO MISTAKE. Doing battle with assholes is risky business. Once they notice your efforts to stifle their rudeness or contempt, they can get mighty riled up and vindictive — and take it out on you. That's why the strategies here for reforming, repelling, defeating, and expelling them require even greater thought and vigilance than those in prior chapters, which focus on escaping or avoiding jerks, or reframing how you think about them, not on challenging and diminishing their influence, prestige, and abuse.

When an asshole problem turns ugly, you may feel agitated and have a burning urge to take down that jerk RIGHT NOW. Yet it's usually smart to squelch your desire for immediate gratification, chill out, and prepare a battle plan. Your instant judgments are likely to be flawed. When the shit hits the fan — even if time is short — finding even a few moments to question your first impulse and to consider other options can avert stupid mistakes. As we saw in chapter 2, Nobel Prize winner Daniel Kahneman warns that when you face a vexing and consequential decision, it's wise to slow down, study your predicament, weigh alternatives, and seek advice from people that you trust before springing into action.

In particular, think about three resources — how much you have and how to get more. The first is how much *power* you have compared to the assholes. The less power you have, the easier it is for jerks to get away with hurting you, the fewer options you have, and more risk you face. The less maneuvering room you have, the more essential it is to take Kahneman's advice about slowing down and squelching your first impulse. Consider an employee who wrote that he was about to lose his job — and asked for advice. A few days earlier, he had told a manager "to go F himself" after the manager had made a derogatory remark about his profession. To make matters worse, he said, the manager "happened to be with his boss and I blasted him as well for allowing this type of conduct to go on."

There wasn't much I could say to help that hothead. It was too late; he had insulted two powerful people. I did urge him to apologize — he was refusing because it was "the asshole who instigated the argument," not him, which further fueled the anger and administrative action that his superiors directed against him. But no matter how demeaning that manager was, it would have been wiser for that employee to hold his temper, to push back in a measured way, and to recruit allies to bolster his power.

Overconfidence is a big roadblock to sound judgments about power. In an interview in the *Guardian* in July of 2015, Kahneman said that overconfidence is the human bias "he would most like to eliminate if he had a magic wand" because it fuels so many terrible decisions. Feeling smug about your capacity to defeat or to banish jerks can be perilous. The new HR head of a *Fortune* 100 company once bragged to me that she was going to fire the firm's most abusive senior executives. When I asked her if it was prudent to move so quickly in her early months on the job, she assured me that the CEO was in her corner and she had a mandate to sack them. She was wrong. The assholes went to the CEO and persuaded him they were less expendable than the HR head — she was canned a few weeks later.

The second resource is *documentation*. The more ironclad your evidence, the easier it is to avert a "he said, she said" situation where it's just your word versus the asshole's. At the first hint of trouble, save your emails and social media exchanges, and keep careful notes — even take pictures and videos if you can. Encourage fellow targets and other allies to do the same. And be careful to follow local laws, as they vary widely. For example, as I write this, California, Florida, and ten or so other U.S. states seem to require "all-party consent"; it's unlawful to record what people say over the phone or in other conversations without their permission. But it appears to be okay to record without others' permission in some forty U.S. states including New York, Colorado, and Virginia.

This advice about documentation is obvious, but many people still don't take it. I've heard from dozens of targets who began documenting too late (or never did), which made it tougher to defend against and to bring down their tormentors. Sound and convincing evidence gives you leverage and legitimacy when you go to the big boss or human resources to complain. And if they give you the brush-off, it gives you ammunition if you seek help from your union, take legal action, or turn to the media. In July 2016, Fox News anchor Gretchen Carlson filed a lawsuit accusing network founder and chairman Roger Ailes — among the most powerful media executives in the world — of forcing her out after she refused his sexual advances and complained about sexism by other Fox colleagues. The suit provoked vehement denials from Ailes, an expression of "full confidence" in him from Fox management, and testimonials about Ailes's sterling character from Fox stars including Brit Hume, Sean Hannity, and Greta Van Susteren.

Yet, within two months, Ailes was out of a job, Fox agreed to a 20-million-dollar settlement with Carlson, and the company made a public apology: "Gretchen was not treated with the respect and dignity that she and all of our colleagues deserve." The lawyers that Fox hired from the prominent firm Paul, Weiss, Rifkind, Wharton & Garrison unearthed extensive evidence of harassment by Ailes; approximately twenty women came forward to report his bad behavior. According to a *New York Times* story in September of 2016, the most damning evidence came from secret recordings that Carlson made on her phone during meetings with Ailes over an eighteen-month stretch. These vile gems included Ailes's suggestion to Carlson, "I think you and I should have had a sexual relationship a long time ago, and then you'd be good and better and I'd be good and better."

That said, there is a downside to becoming fixated on cataloging every slight and insult and pressing others to document abuse and to share their evidence with you. In academic speak, it's "nonclinical paranoia," which is "a form of heightened and exaggerated distrust" including "perceptions of being threatened, harmed, persecuted, mistreated, disparaged, and so on, by malevolent others." Researchers MeowLan Evelyn Chan and Daniel McAllister contend that when employees distrust others too much and are flooded with fear and anxiety, they become excessively vigilant, focus on just the bad and tune out the good, and see evil motives in the most innocent actions. If you become obsessed with gathering every crumb of evidence about bullying, you risk manufacturing a monster in your mind — construing actions by alleged bullies as being more sinister than warranted and blinding yourself to any good that they do.

Yet the expression "just because you're paranoid doesn't mean that they aren't out to get you" is sometimes true. My Stanford colleague Rod Kramer points to author Ernest Hemingway, who was convinced that the FBI was following him for years, his phone was tapped, and agents intercepted his mail. Hemingway complained about, and sometimes confronted, men in dark suits that he encountered in bars and restaurants that he suspected were spying on him. Friends and family struggled to reassure him they were just regular people and the FBI wasn't out to get him. Psychiatrists who treated Hemingway saw this obsession as indicative of "clinical paranoia." But Hemingway was right. In 1942, Bureau chief J. Edgar Hoover launched an "intense program of surveillance" of the famed author, which persisted until his suicide in 1961. When Hemingway was hospitalized in 1960 (and given electric shock treatments for depression), he complained to doctors that the clicking noises on his phone meant the FBI was listening—which the doctors saw as further evidence of his paranoia. Perhaps it was, but Hemingway's extensive FBI file (released under the U.S. Freedom of Information Act) reveals that the FBI did tap that phone.

The third resource pops up throughout this book, that of *unity or solidarity*. Sometimes you must fight alone, but you have a better chance of winning when others join you. When you have allies, you have more power, you can encourage each other to keep fighting during tough times, and it's easier to convince skeptics you aren't a lone or singular nut (which was part of Hemingway's problem).

A study by Professor Pamela Lutgen-Sandvik found that when bullied employees banded together to fight back, authorities punished 58% of the abusers and none of the bullied employees were fired. But when employees battled alone, only 27% of the bullies were punished and 20% of the bullied employees were fired. For example, Lutgen-Sandvik reported how, after a few teachers told a school board member about an abusive administrator, the floodgates opened, and many victims came forward. A teacher explained:

It's like when the little boys who are sexually abused by the priests . . . when one of them speaks out, all the others come out of the woodwork? Well, it was like that. Once we talked to Bob [on school board], a lot of other teachers got up the courage to join in and say, "Hey it's not okay." You know what I mean? They weren't so scared anymore.

People who were bullied by your tormentor in the past but have escaped the abuse can be especially valuable supporters. An ethics professor wrote me that when graduate students and postdoctoral fellows ask him about dealing with nasty and unethical bosses at his university, he suggests they contact "anyone else who knows the asshole" because they "are your natural allies." The professor described a postdoctoral student who contacted one of his terrible boss's former underlings — this fellow victim offered emotional support, joined him in registering complaints with administrators about the boss (who also took steps to protect the postdoc), and helped the student move to a better position in another lab.

Now let's turn to strategies for battling assholes; I'll talk about how and when to use them, why they work (and sometimes don't), and harken back to those three key resources along the way.

Calm, rational, and candid confrontation.   This is a civilized way to fight. You pull the offenders aside and calmly, even gently, explain they are hurting you or others — and ask them to knock it off. As chapter 7 will show, we humans are cursed with a dim awareness of how our actions are experienced by and impact others. Controlled, candid, and negative feedback can rattle and reform jerks who are afflicted with big blind spots. This approach works well with temporary or clueless assholes, when you have a trusted relationship with them, or if you wield power over them. And it works best with people who pride themselves on being civil — and cringe at the thought of others calling them assholes behind their backs. The well-meaning but clueless CEO of one company that I know was horrified when two female executive vice presidents pulled him aside and gently admonished him after a meeting. The women — who kept careful tallies — informed the CEO he had interrupted each of them at least six times but never interrupted the four male executive vice presidents. Stunned and embarrassed, the CEO begged for forgiveness, asked them to keep tracking his interruptions, and vowed to halt his sexist ways. He didn't want to feel that self-loathing again.

Staying calm and civil can be effective with less admirable culprits too. But you might need to turn up the heat a bit to get their attention. A manager at a large public utility wrote me that his workplace was filled with assholes despite strong talk from executives about adhering to the company's "core values," which were plastered on the walls and website. The manager often observed gaps between such soaring rhetoric and the various indignities heaped on employees — so he invoked the values whenever colleagues violated them.

He described a compensation review meeting with fellow managers one year when budgets were tight, where they discussed how much to pay people. One of his nastier colleagues said, "They should just be grateful to have a job." The manager was polite but pushed back: "Nice, can you tell me which core value that represents — is it integrity, respect, maybe teamwork? No, seriously . . . I would like to know how that fits into the overall direction of the company and how we are going to communicate this to our employees and rate payers." He went on to explain, "I find that if you take the opportunity to throw out a subtle reminder of the core values we are required to adhere to, the a**hole quickly backs up, swallows the words, and rethinks the tactic."

Finally, consider the letter that British prime minister Winston Churchill received from his wife Clementine on June 27, 1940 — when news about World War II was getting worse and worse for the United Kingdom and Churchill was taking out his angst on his staff. Clementine wrote: "One of the men in your entourage (a devoted friend) has been to me & told me that there is a danger of your being generally disliked by your colleagues and subordinates because of your rough sarcastic & overbearing manner." After spelling out some ugly details, Clementine added, "I was astonished & upset because in all these years I have been accustomed to all those who have worked with & under you, loving you." And then, "My Darling Winston — I must confess that I have noticed a deterioration in your manner; & you are not so kind as you used to be." She advised, "With this terrific power you must combine urbanity, kindness and if possible Olympic calm." Clementine ended, "Besides you won't get the best results by irascibility & rudeness. They will breed either dislike or a slave mentality."

These three examples are varied but share two elements of effective confrontations — which may even hold when the encounter turns loud and angry rather than calm. Research on "moral anger" and "righteous anger" suggests that confrontation is most likely to reform offenders, be seen as socially acceptable, and mobilize support when:

1. It is justified — there is good evidence that the person is doing something bad.

2. The motivation for the confrontation is seen as constructive and aimed at improving the greater good; not just a selfish, vindictive, or irrational urge to inflict harm on an enemy or nemesis.

That marvelous letter from Clementine to Winston Churchill illustrates both principles. First, she knew that Winston's "irascibility & rudeness" was getting worse from her experience with him and information from her "devoted friend" including that "if an idea is suggested (say at a conference) you are supposed to be so contemptuous that presently no ideas, good or bad, will be forthcoming." Second, her motivation was to help the staff, England, and its allies. Clementine's letter was written largely on behalf of others who lacked the power that she wielded over Winston. And her postscript conveys that her criticism wasn't a rash decision: "I wrote this at Chequers last Sunday, tore it up, but here it is now."

Aggressive confrontation.   It's usually a bad idea to call someone an "asshole" — especially in anger and in the presence of others. No matter how accurate the label might be, it will probably be taken as an asshole move on your part. For example, a former home improvement store employee wrote me that she was fired after calling a coworker an "asshole." She asked me to urge her bosses to reverse the decision because, after all, she was just enforcing the no asshole rule. I declined. Applying, and especially saying, the word to people who offend you is not only usually rude; it's like throwing gasoline on a fire — it can ignite even more ornery and obnoxious behavior. Mennonite pastor Arthur Paul Boers offers similar advice in his book *Never Call Them Jerks*. Boers suggests that when parishioners are hostile and selfish, labeling them as jerks is insulting and detracts from a constructive focus on repairing relationships and changing behavior.

Yet there is evidence that when dealing with certain kinds of selfish jerks, returning their fire can work (although I suggest using something more civil than "you asshole"). You need to convince some people that you aren't a doormat and won't let them push you around, or they may turn even more nasty and selfish. They take your kindness as a symptom of weakness. A 2015 study by Hungarian researchers found that people with Machiavellian personalities — selfish individuals who "consider other people as mere tools to be leveraged in the pursuit of their aims" — have brains that go into "overdrive" when they work with "fair and cooperative" people. These malicious takers immediately start conniving to exploit people for their own purposes — but back off when they encounter uncooperative and selfish people like themselves.

Related research suggests that pushing back hard — glaring, raising your voice, making threats, even throwing a tantrum — is useful for fending off characters who believe they can get ahead by stomping on others' feelings and reputations. My Stanford colleague Rod Kramer calls this "porcupine power." A manager wrote me about how returning fire deterred "a major asshole" that she worked with (a retired army major who was infamous for his insults and disrespect). She tried to be nice to him at first. But he belittled her more and started poaching her people and her budget for his projects. The manager realized that he took her warmth and cooperation as signs of weakness. She then went to his office, gave him "a hard stare" and informed him that such behavior was "absolutely unacceptable" and she simply wouldn't tolerate it. The retired major backed off. Porcupine power was the only language he understood.

When you are dealing with a pushy jerk who is undermining the greater good, even if they wield power over you, a flash of righteous anger can sometimes get them to back down. The lead engineer for a software company's "premier product" wrote me that, at 6:30 one evening, his team was wrapping the "final build" before an update was released. The CEO's "right-hand man" rushed in and was "ACTUALLY FLAPPING HIS ARMS." The "right-hand man" told the team that the company couldn't release the software until they reviewed some new documentation. The lead engineer told him it would take the team about 20 minutes to do so. This provoked "a self-important rant about how it couldn't take 20 minutes because he was the CEO's right-hand man" and must be done faster. As the lead engineer tells it:

> *My whole team was clustered in the hall behind the ranter looking over his shoulder at me, trying to see what I was going to do. The ranter continued, saying how important it was to get it done fast and sooner and how urgent it was not to stop the software release because he'd already told the CEO that all the release steps were done. When he finished ranting, I continued to look him straight in the eye and said, "Twenty-five minutes," and shut the door in his face.*

When the lead engineer slammed that door, he expressed righteous anger for the greater good of his team and the company (although he clearly took pleasure in bringing down the "right-hand man" a notch). And his team loved him for it.

There are other times when subtle "passive-aggressive" confrontation is best for conveying the thought, "You are acting like a jerk and I want you to stop." After all, in some organizational and national cultures, direct confrontation is frowned upon. And when you have brief encounters with rude people — be it a customer, someone you don't know at your place of worship, or someone at a restaurant, theater, or a sporting event — asking them to keep it down, saying "shush," and glaring can fail or backfire because you have no prior relationship with them. A reader sent me a great story about a bunch of people behind him, talking through the movie, "making fun of things, generally being distracting" when he and a friend went to see *Live Free or Die Hard*. He tried "the usual thing" of turning around and glaring at them, but it didn't work. Finally, "During one longer, quiet stretch, I turned to my friend next to me and said, pretty loudly, 'So, what do YOU want to talk about?' and he said, also loudly, 'I don't know, why don't we wait until later?'" He reported, "It worked — the people behind us remained silent through the rest of the picture." This method delivered the message to those clueless assholes to pipe down and it "was kind of funny, and didn't lead to any escalation."

As noted in chapter 5, insults and put-downs wrapped in humor may hit harder — and be more socially acceptable — than those delivered in serious ways. Targets also can use humor to battle bad behavior — as happened in that movie theater with that passive-aggressive move. When you are peppered with cruel humor, firing back with cutting and funny words can foil attackers, especially if the bullies take you for a doormat who they can tease and belittle at will.

A high school teacher wrote me that a colleague finally toned down his taunting after she learned to "throw it back at him in ways that made everyone laugh." She developed a "stockpile of comebacks" that, she said, "seemed like jokes, but I wasn't joking" including, "You are so cute when you are polite" and "Are you always this nice, or do you single me out because I am so special?" Of course, cutting and sarcastic humor is risky. Just like any move that entails throwing shit at others, it can ignite a vicious circle. And if you have less power, your snappy comebacks can motivate jerks to exact revenge. Yet, in some places, what may seem like rough joking, teasing, and put-downs to outsiders is accepted and expected. When aggressive humor, or "trash talk," is the norm, people who wield power don't just dish it out; they expect it and enjoy it when others throw it back. And when top dogs go too far, when they leave others feeling demeaned, people know that a joke or a prank is the best way to deliver the message to back off.

A tough former Silicon Valley CEO told me a story about how his team made him the butt of a joke — and how it reduced tension on the team, brought them closer together, and conveyed that he should turn down his hostility. For some reason, many of the insults he aimed at senior executives entailed unfavorable comparisons to vegetables, such as "you are dumber than a head of lettuce" or "the average zucchini could figure this out."

His team cooked up some payback. One day, when the CEO walked into the conference room for a meeting, instead of seeing people at their usual places, each team member was replaced with a head of lettuce on the table next to his or her chair. There was even a head of lettuce next to the CEO's chair at the head of the table. The CEO sent me a picture — each of the eleven lettuce heads on the table has eyes and a smile drawn on it; most have hats and some have sunglasses. He added, "They made a lettuce head T-shirt too, which many of us wore on a regular basis." The CEO admitted there were times when he was too hard on his team, but he emphasized his company had changed and grown so fast that survival required mental toughness. In just a few years, his team led the company from a struggling start-up to one of the fastest-growing companies in Silicon Valley, and on through a successful public offering. People who were ready for this wild ride not only could tolerate his sometimes rude humor, but they had the confidence to throw it back —and the give-and-take brought them all closer together. He admitted, however, that after the lettuce incident, he did pause a bit before using vegetable humor or saying other things that could bruise people's feelings.

Love bombing and ass-kissing.   Buttering up people who treat you like dirt may seem like an odd battle plan. But flattery, smiles, and other signs of appreciation (even if not entirely sincere) can be useful for convincing volatile and vindictive people to tamp down their inner angst and anger — so they won't take it out on you. A software engineer wrote me that she studies the local jerks to learn how to "make them happier in small ways" and "play to their weaknesses." She described a quality assurance person on her team who was "notorious for her short temper under stress." As the release date for a product approached, and the stress amplified, she launched withering attacks on colleagues (without ever swearing) that made clear "you had a level of brain power and industry understanding slightly below that of an amoeba." The engineer then noticed something useful:

> *I learned — by observation — that she loved chocolate, especially dark chocolate, and that she tended to comfort eat under stress, and it helped. And so, as the tension ratcheted up each release cycle, I'd bring in a couple pounds of Hershey's (or seasonally appropriate candy if it was near a holiday), making sure there was some dark chocolate among it, and put it in*

the lab for all the QA folks . . . it really could blunt the worst of her temper.

Such "chocolate bombing" is a subtle and indirect version of this strategy. Sometimes more intense love bombing (and ass-kissing too) is called for, and can be mighty effective when paired with more aggressive strategies. It's handy for keeping an insensitive or narcissistic jerk at bay while you prepare a sneak attack. Narcissists crave constant praise and flattery; they desperately need to believe they are beloved. Although narcissists are often abusive and insulting, they are thin-skinned and don't tolerate people who are even mildly unpleasant to them or who question their judgment.

Michael Maccoby, who has studied and coached narcissistic leaders for decades, observes that they "often say that they want teamwork, what that means in practice is that they want a group of yes-men." My advice may sound unsavory, even hypocritical. But if you want protection from powerful and prickly narcissists, there is an argument for kissing up in order to provide cover and to keep them calm while you work backstage to bring them down.

A community college administrator told me a long story about how his former chancellor demanded complete loyalty and if his staff didn't "stroke his ego constantly," he was prone to fly into a rage. This administrator and several colleagues spent a year assembling an ironclad case against their boss — they meticulously documented his terrible judgment, his insatiable need for praise, his penchant for belittling others, and his temper tantrums. They turned in their evidence to the trustees, who eventually fired him. The administrator explained that he and his fellow "turncoats" gave the chancellor his daily dose of fawning and false flattery because it helped stem his narcissistic rages while they hatched their plot.

Other studies suggest that some people are grumpy, insulting, or overbearing primarily because they are insecure about their abilities and prestige. This is a hallmark of petty tyrants, which I discussed in chapter 2 — those masters of small domains who lord their power over others in narrow-minded, demeaning, and sometimes silly ways. Unlike narcissists, most petty tyrants don't crave or expect admiration or flattery, but they do take solace in imposing their will on others and making them miserable. An engineer wrote me he's found that many "assholes are simply afraid of (or for) something. They are typically the lesser lords of the castle, hiding behind or upon its walls and moat, looking down on all the dangerous creatures roaming the air-conditioned countryside surrounding their little office domain. The asshole's default action is to pour burning oil down upon any who dare approach the gate." The engineer said his solution is to orient himself "as a comrade inside of the walls, therefore bypassing the confrontation." He avoids the asshole's wrath by expressing empathy and finding common ground — shared interests such as hobbies, sports, or politics ("It cannot include deviant action like kicking puppies or spying on coworkers"). He said this approach works about "seven out of ten times," and by holding his tongue and expressing empathy rather than anger, he not only avoids the jerk's wrath; he lowers his own "asshole potential" as well.

"Love bombing" is a related and more extreme strategy for dealing with insecure assholes — you go beyond expressing empathy and holding your tongue, and respond to their nastiness with warmth and kindness. Your aim is to transform your oppressor into a friend and admirer. I got this idea from my daughter Claire, who worked with a grumpy tyrant when she was a hostess in a tequila bar and restaurant in Boston. The cook glared and growled at her and the servers night after night. Claire decided to "kill him with kindness."

No matter how unpleasant the cook was, she smiled at him, offered compliments about his great food and how hard he worked, and responded to his barbs with warmth and understanding. This "love bombing" eventually "wore him down" and within a few months, she said, "He was very nice to me and even gave me free food." Claire added, "He was just a guy who needed a friend."

Revenge is sweet, but can be useless and dangerous.   Fighting and defeating assholes can satisfy the all-too-human desire for revenge. As Eric Jaffe's essay on "The Complicated Psychology of Revenge" put it: "A thirst for vengeance is nothing if not timeless. It is as classic as Homer and Hamlet, and as contemporary as Don Corleone and Quentin Tarantino; as old as the eyes and teeth traded in the Bible." The desire for "payback" and associated righteous anger can bond people together who are bent on bringing down a common enemy — as with those college administrators who ambushed their chancellor. Skilled confrontation can be similarly satisfying — like that lead engineer who slammed the door on the "ranter," bought his team twenty-five more minutes, and took down "the CEO's right-hand man" a notch. Or readers of *The No Asshole Rule* may recall the radio station producer who got back at a demeaning boss who kept stealing her food. She made some chocolates out of Ex-Lax, the laxative, and left them on her desk. Then, "Sure enough, her boss came by and devoured them without asking permission. When she told him what was in them, 'he was not happy.'" But he stopped stealing her food.

These examples dovetail with findings from a study by Columbia University's Harvey Hornstein. His conclusion after interviewing one hundred employees about dealing with abusive bosses was, "Successful payback is *well-targeted* (aimed at the abuser), *well-timed* (occurring at times that established a connection between the abuse and the payback), and *well-tempered* (motivated and crafted to end the abuse rather than merely inflict cost)." Hornstein labels vengeful acts as failures when they don't change the perpetrator's behavior —but such payback may still help targets by bolstering feelings that they aren't helpless doormats.

Consider one of my favorite revenge stories. It's from the *Wall Street Journal's* Jason Zweig. He was standing in the check-in line at New York's Kennedy Airport. The passenger in front of him went on and on berating and insulting an airline employee. Jason was struck by the employee's ability to remain cool and professional in the face of the onslaught. Jason wrote me, "It is her words that have stuck forever in my memory: 'Oh, he's going to [L.A.], but his luggage is going to Nairobi' — and the faint but unmistakable firmness in her smile that made me realize, half with a chill and half with a thrill, that she wasn't kidding." Sneaky revenge moves like these don't change behavior but may enable targets to take a bit of control, get something from their tormentor, and garner respect and kudos from witnesses.

Yet revenge is treacherous. Hornstein found that 68% of the payback efforts that he studied failed to stop abusive bosses. As we saw in chapter 5, research on schoolyard and workplace bullying shows that people who ruminate about getting even, rather than letting it go, suffer negative effects including anxiety, depression, and sleep problems. Revenge fantasies might be fun to talk about, but I worry when people who escape an asshole are still obsessed with payback months and years later. A former assembly worker wrote me that she couldn't stop thinking about an awful boss who constantly spied on her, criticized her, and wrote her up for trivial violations. She sent me multiple long emails filled with pranks that she fantasized about pulling on him — such as changing all the locks in his house, gluing his windows shut, unplugging his refrigerator, and jamming the electric meter, and after four to five months, calling the fraud unit at the electric company. That bosshole was still in her head and driving her crazy, even though she had parted company with him years before.

As much as I love Jason's airport story, Hornstein found that when secret revenge inflicts harm on clients, colleagues, or organizations, it might make you feel good for a while. But in the end, it doesn't change the bad behavior. Hornstein describes a payback campaign by Julie (an insurance company employee) after a new boss had criticized Julie's work at a meeting with several colleagues and then she added, "There's just no explanation except laziness or lack of ability." Julie was humiliated and mad, and exacted revenge by repeatedly altering and deleting files on her boss's computer. This sabotage slowed Julie's boss's work, frustrated her, and made her look bad. As Julie admitted, "It was childish and vicious." The boss never caught Julie, but she lost in other ways — she was consumed with thoughts of revenge, it slowed her organization's work, and it didn't stop the abuse.

Julie and others who exact revenge may believe it will bolster their spirits, but experiments led by Colgate University's Kevin Carlsmith suggest otherwise. His research team had contestants play an interactive "prisoner's dilemma" game that, in essence, was rigged so that one player was a selfish and deceitful villain who screwed everyone else. After urging fellow contestants to cooperate so that each could win a moderate amount of money, the planted villain screwed them all at the end of the game to win the lion's share of the prize money.

Some participants were given the chance to "punish" this selfish jerk with financial penalties — and nearly always elected to exact revenge. The most interesting group, however, contained people who were screwed too, but didn't have any means to punish the jerk — they didn't get to exact revenge because the experimenters made it impossible for them to do so. They experienced weaker and shorter-lasting negative emotions than contestants who could and did get revenge, which was exactly the opposite of what most people would predict (including participants in this study). Carlsmith explained, "In actuality punishers ruminate on their deed and feel worse than those who cannot avenge a wrong," and people "who don't have a chance to take revenge are forced, in a sense, to move on and focus on something different." Carlsmith's team concluded that Sir Francis Bacon might have been right when, some four centuries ago, he wrote, "A man that studieth revenge, keeps his own wounds green, which otherwise would heal, and do well."

Carlsmith's revenge experiments examined brief episodes — the game, transgression, revenge (or not), reaction, and rumination were all over in an hour. Payback may have different long-term consequences, especially if it is felt by and can change an asshole's future behavior. As Hornstein's study showed, revenge can be beneficial when it slows or stops persistent abuse.

But revenge can also fuel endless ugliness. Revenge researchers Robert Bies and Thomas Tripp found that the impulse to "get even" can provoke a vicious circle of attack and counterattack — where each side views the other as evil and won't accept responsibility for fueling the conflict, and "both sides view their own actions as purely defensive behaviors made in response to the other's unwarranted actions." If you are locked in such an ugly tit-for-tat game, one that rages for months or years, you not only are hurting yourself and your nemesis; you are also dragging others down with you.

A few years ago, I had a long conversation with a consultant who described how the simmering jealousy and anger between two of his firm's rainmakers had exploded into open warfare. Their back-stage bad-mouthing and open confrontations were driving away clients and causing some of his favorite colleagues to jump ship. And the physical health of the two warring partners was degenerating too. The consultant had wise words about that shit fight, along the lines of "It is like when your mother and father are fighting. You don't care who is right or wrong. You just want them to stop." If you are trapped in one of these brutal cycles, remember the research in chapter 5 on forgiveness. Even if your tormentors don't deserve it, finding it in your heart to forgive them might be best for you, for those you care about, and for those unworthy jerks too.

Use the system to reform, defeat, and expel jerks.   In *The No Asshole Rule,* I described how to design and build organizations that don't tolerate members, customers, students, or volunteers who leave others feeling disrespected, demeaned, and de-energized. I showed how organizations that enforce this rule actively recruit civilized people, teach them to treat others with respect, reward and give power to people who exhibit such behavior, and punish and eventually expel those who persistently break the rule. I've heard from and about dozens of organizations with "no asshole" or "no jerks" rules, including Baird (financial services), Concertia (cloud computing and hosting), Box (file sharing), Eventbrite (online ticket sales and event organizing), Invoice2go (invoicing for small businesses), Royal Bank of Canada, J. Walter Thompson Worldwide (a big advertising agency), and Netflix, where Patty McCord (who led the "People Department" there for fourteen years) told me she was proud of the mantra they built the company culture around: "no bozos, no assholes."

In a team or organization that lives the rule, the system helps people battle jerks whether they are at the bottom, middle, or top of the pecking order. Some of the best leaders and teams don't talk about it; they just apply it. And it isn't necessarily something that comes from on high — you can band together with peers to enforce the rule in your corner of the world. Here's how a reader and his colleagues did it:

> *Assholes are like cockroaches. If you shine a light on them, they run for cover. At our workplace, we're starting to insist on more transparency, less backroom chatter, and an end to the secrecy that allows our resident asshole to carry on his antics. We share information with each other, refuse to let him trap us into private discussions of our coworkers, and generally don't give him permission to manipulate us. It's driving him nuts! He's run out of allies (who were never very willing to begin with), and he doesn't know what to do next.*

It's difficult for bullies to do dirty work when they are surrounded with people who hold them accountable and who share information about their abuse. Skilled tormentors and backstabbers may get away with concealing their moves from a boss or two — often by kissing up to superiors and kicking everyone else. But it's a lot harder to get away with it when everyone you encounter tries to stop you. As Huggy Rao and I wrote in *Scaling Up Excellence,* in places with high accountability, destructive characters can't hide because everybody acts like "I own the place and it owns me."

If you are at or near the top of the pecking order, you have a big, big impact on whether people feel safe turning to the system for protection or if they see leaders like you as jerks, hypocrites, or both. First, you've got to nip bad behavior in the bud. As psychologist Roy

Baumeister and his colleagues show in their article "Bad Is Stronger Than Good," negative behaviors such as cheating, laziness, grumpiness, anger, and disrespect — you name it — pack a bigger wallop, are more contagious, and are much harder to stop than good behaviors. When employees have negative interactions with supervisors, for example, it has five times more impact on their moods than positive interactions. And Will Felps's research on "bad apples" found that when a team has even just one deadbeat or jerk, performance drops by 30% to 40%. The longer you wait, the worse it gets.

The former CEO of a Canadian start-up wrote me, "Our company was filled with assholes from the directors on down to our sales people." For years, he fought their disrespect and unethical acts. Yet the assholes hired more assholes and the maliciousness spread. In the end, they ganged up on the CEO and convinced the board to fire him. He said, "My biggest mistake was not firing the assholes fast enough and my compassion got the better of me." In contrast, Paul Purcell, Chairman of Baird, doesn't just talk about nipping bad behavior in the bud. Paul told me he informs job candidates that if he discovers they are assholes, he will fire them. And he has done so on several occasions. Paul believes that living the no asshole rule has helped fuel Baird's persistent financial success, growth, and selection as one of *Fortune*'s "100 Best Companies to Work For" every year since 2004 (they were ranked fourth in 2017).

Second, I am all for firing people who are persistently demeaning, become violent, or display extreme cruelty. But if you want to make a place safe for people to take on culprits, and admit their own bad behaviors too, it's crucial to treat alleged jerks with dignity and respect. That means starting with calm and backstage conversations with them and giving them chances to change. It also means realizing that some people aren't usually jerks, but there is something about the characters they work with, their customers, or the work they do that brings out their worst selves. Moving them to another location or team can spark big improvements.

Laszlo Bock, who headed Google's "People Operations" teams for a decade, documents the virtues of a change of scene. In *Work Rules!* he reports that when a Googler is at the bottom of the performance curve, the lower 5%, the company gives them that negative feedback — but doesn't fire them right away. They wait to avoid stoking fear and because many of these employees are salvageable. When such struggling employees move to another role at Google, their performance typically rises to about the average level in the company. As Bock explains, moving from the 5th to 50th percentile isn't just good for the salvaged employee; it helps Google because finding, recruiting, and onboarding replacements takes a lot of time and money. Bock's evidence isn't about assholes in particular; but treating others with dignity and respect is factored into the hiring and assessment of every Googler. Indeed, Bock tells me that many employees who are ranked in the bottom 5% not only don't realize that they are performing so badly; they also are clueless about the negative impact they're having on the people around them. That "telling them where they stand, while giving them the chance to try a new environment, is often enough to get them to change their behavior."

My Stanford colleague Perry Klebahn uses a similar method. He's found that moving overbearing jerks to different teams can sometimes bring out the good in them and also free others from their wrath. I've been teaching innovation classes with Perry at the Institute of Design at Stanford (everyone calls it "the d.school") for over a decade, including hands-on programs where we put forty to sixty visiting executives into five- or six-person teams. These pressure-packed three-to-five-day projects have included improving the "airport experience" for JetBlue passengers, making a visit to the Stanford Blood Bank more comforting and inspiring for donors, and improving the customer experience at BP gas stations.

Each team of executives does on-site observations and interviews, generates solutions, develops prototypes, tests them with users, and — as the grand finale — presents their best prototype to leaders at the "client" organization and the teaching team. Every team has a coach that guides them through each step. As a program unfolds, Perry and colleague Jeremy Utley watch each team closely: They constantly check in with coaches and jump in to help troubled teams. Each night, Perry and Jeremy debrief with the coaches to discuss what is working, what is not, and what repairs they might make.

As Huggy Rao and I reported in *Scaling Up Excellence,* once or twice a year, a few teams are infected with what Perry calls "alpha types" with "big personalities." I call them assholes. Perry "puts all the bad apples in one barrel" so they don't wreck other teams. He then assigns a no-nonsense coach to lead the bad apples or does it himself — he is adept at dispensing tough love. It works. Teams that lose the alphas often express relief and do better work. Plus it's easier for the teaching team to deal with the jerks when they are all in one place.

Perry reports that one or two "bad apple teams" have been plagued by conflict and done poor work; but most develop healthy dynamics and produce "shockingly good prototypes." Perry's method requires exercising power over assholes. But you might be able to entice them to gather together in one group or place. As Robert Cialdini shows in his classic book *Influence,* similar people are attracted to each other and enjoy spending time together. In fact, Perry believes one reason bad apple teams usually do such good work is that members appreciate and understand fellow "alpha types."

Third, and finally, if you want people to believe the system is fair and effective, it's essential to be tough on the most powerful, profitable, and well-known jerks. If you enforce the rule only with the weak performers, people who are easily replaceable, or who deliver bad news and have the gumption to disagree with superiors — and you allow powerful assholes to run roughshod over anyone they please — people will smell your hypocritical bullshit from a mile away. In chapter 2, I discussed how leaders including Rob Fyfe from Air New Zealand protected employees and gained their trust by firing nasty customers and clients. It takes particular courage to fire a big client when your organization depends on only a few to survive.

That's what CEO Bill Carmody did in 2008 right after he launched Trepoint, a digital marketing company. A potential new client from a big company had contacted Carmody: As *Huffington Post* blogger Molly Reynolds reported, if Trepoint could have landed the work, it would have provided a huge boost to the start-up. Carmody's team worked long hours to develop a proposal and pitch with just the right "wow factor" for the client. Unfortunately, when they presented it to an executive from the big company, he wasn't just critical; he totally "berated Bill's staff" and was "borderline abusive." Carmody stood up and told the potential client: "We're not the right firm for you . . . I don't allow this type of treatment to my staff. We're happy to refer you to another company who might accommodate you."

Carmody later told his shocked staff, "Even if you satisfy their needs, assholes attract more assholes, and I'm not subjecting you guys to that." That philosophy, for both clients and employees, is one reason that Carmody believes his company is growing and attracting great people — it has bustling offices in Kansas City, New York, and San Francisco and is on *Inc.*'s list of the fastest-growing private companies.

Alas, bosses like Bill Carmody are rare. Too many leaders and systems don't protect people from these powerful jerks or — worse — throw those with the courage to fight them under the bus.

A warning about weak or rigged systems.   During the past decade or so, the litany of bad news about workplace bullying, harassment, and bias against women, lesbian, gay, bisexual, and transgender people, and members of various religious groups has provoked politicians, lawyers, regulators, corporate leaders, and other anti-asshole crusaders to propose (and sometimes implement) legal solutions. Anti-bullying laws that protect schoolkids have been adopted in fifty U.S. states. The Joint Commission's 2008 standards require all 5,600 U.S. hospitals to "have a code of conduct as well as a process for managing disruptive and inappropriate behaviors." These rules could have some bite because the Joint Commission is the main organization that accredits and certifies health-care organizations and programs in the United States. The commission's medical director Ronald Wyatt justified these rules in a 2013 post on their *Leadership Blog.* He cited evidence that doctors who are uncooperative, use "condescending language or voice intonation," and take "overt actions such as verbal outbursts and physical threats" intimidate fellow health-care workers, which, in turn, contributes "directly to medical errors."

Yet as much as I admire many of these crusaders for laws, rules, and regulations, and sometimes fancy myself as one, I am wary of legal solutions. Sure, they work sometimes. This is especially true if you've got a very strong case and an expensive lawyer, as Gretchen Carlson did when she sued Fox News. But recall that she claims to have endured years of sexual harassment before taking legal action.

If you examine the widespread anti-bullying laws for protecting schoolkids, for example, they are pretty weak. Most simply require schools to have a written anti-bullying policy—which is hollow rhetoric without the right leaders, culture, and resources to instill and enforce them day after day. Indeed, there is little evidence that these laws have reduced bullying in schools: in 2014, UCLA professors Jaana Juvonen and Sandra Graham reviewed 140 studies and found that the anti-bullying programs used in most schools are weak and ineffective for protecting victims or punishing culprits.

Moreover, as of October 2016, workplace bullying remained LEGAL in all fifty U.S. states, as the Workplace Bullying Institute's detailed and useful website points out (the institute is led by Gary Namie, a relentless advocate against workplace bullying). In other words, in the United States, it isn't against the law to be an equal opportunity asshole—one who treats everyone like dirt regardless of their background. The institute's website advises that if you are in a "protected" group based on factors including gender, race, religion, and age, you might be able to use federal civil rights laws to fight back. But the institute's surveys show that such discriminatory harassment occurs in only about 20% of bullying cases. The institute goes on to warn victims who are contemplating legal action: "Depositions (intense invasive interrogations) by the employer's attorneys re-traumatized injured bullied workers. Many quit their lawsuits at that stage. Your privacy will be lost. Your health records will be available for your bully and employer to mock . . . If you are even considering a lawsuit, you face a tough road of personalized hate directed at you."

As I've emphasized, even if your organization has "official" systems, practices, and written values in place to prevent abusive and disrespectful behavior, that doesn't mean that people in HR, legal, or senior management will help you fight the local bullies. Yes, sometimes, such systems are effective. Baird, Google, and Bill Carmody's Trepoint all appear to have leaders who espouse and enforce such standards. And recall "the Sea Witch" Captain Holly Graf of the U.S. Navy from chapter 2: Graf's malicious words and deeds prompted numerous complaints and a thorough investigation, and she was ultimately relieved of her command. Too often, however, even when such systems exist, it's risky to use them to battle powerful assholes. Just raising the issue of abuse can get you branded as a troublemaker. And if you are going after influential and politically adept people, even if they are beneath you in the official pecking order, they can rally their allies against you.

A supervisor wrote me that one of her direct reports — the department secretary — was "nasty, mean, and insubordinate" whenever they were alone, but "sweet as sugar" when others were present. Her surly secretary had cultivated a close friendship with the human resources director. The supervisor explained the two "go out to dinner together and help each other with personal stuff." As a result, the supervisor's efforts to document and report the secretary's surliness (and incompetence) was all for naught. The secretary denied it all and (with help from her powerful friend in HR) escaped punishment.

Lance Armstrong provides a textbook case of how a powerful and sleazy asshole can make life miserable for anybody who dares to reveal the ugly truth. This seven-time winner of the Tour de France bicycle race was eventually stripped of his titles for using banned substances and blood doping. After denying any wrongdoing for years, he finally admitted his sins on Oprah Winfrey's TV show on January 17, 2013 — confessing that he used banned substances and methods in every victory, which included testosterone, cortisone, human growth hormone, and blood transfusions. Armstrong is now reviled as a liar and a cheater. But the damage that this rich, arrogant, and vindictive creep did to teammates, journalists, former friends, and anyone else who revealed his cheating — or just asked questions about it — was breathtaking. Armstrong and his lawyers sued people who told the truth, called them liars and lowlifes, and ruined their reputations and careers.

For example, Armstrong received a settlement of about $500,000 from the *Sunday Times* of London in 2006 after they ran stories by David Walsh that accused him of doping. As Walsh reported in the same newspaper in January 2013, Armstrong bashed him as a "scumbag" and a "liar." He said, "Walsh is the worst journalist I know." Lawsuits and personal attacks like these caused other journalists to avoid asking Armstrong tough questions or to write stories about his doping. After Armstrong's lies were exposed, the *Sunday Times* sued him for over a million dollars and announced in August 2013 that they were "entirely happy" with the confidential financial settlement. Walsh was vindicated and won kudos in the United Kingdom, including Journalist of the Year in 2012 and the Barclays Lifetime Achievement Award for journalism in 2013.

As the *New York Times* wrote in January 2013, Armstrong also made threats and degrading comments about Betsy Andreu for years (a teammate's wife who testified that Armstrong admitted to taking steroids in her presence). Armstrong also called former team masseuse Emma O'Reilly a prostitute and alcoholic after she admitted to transporting drugs for Armstrong's team and getting rid of the evidence. Armstrong sued O'Reilly too. He dropped the lawsuit in 2006. But as the *New York Daily News* reported in October 2012, O'Reilly lamented that "the damage Lance caused to my reputation still remains." In the end, Armstrong was brought down, but many who stood up to him paid a steep price.

Public figures or executives aren't the only dangerous assholes. As we've seen, such jerks don't need to hold prestigious positions — they just need to be adept at recruiting allies to help them backstab, intimidate, and spread vicious lies about anybody who stands in their way. Unfortunately, targets oppressed by such people often have sound reasons for remaining silent and enduring the abuse. I don't condone it, but it's easy to understand why victims trapped in these terrible situations tell lies about an asshole's cruel and sleazy words and deeds — as many people around Lance Armstrong did to protect their own livelihoods and avoid his vengeance. I believe in doing battle when you have a decent chance to win, or even when the odds are low, but only when the people you take on have neither the means nor inclination to do serious harm to you. Alas, sometimes it's wiser and safer to lay low, to say nothing, and to wait for the opportunity to get the hell out.

A BATTLE FOR YOUR DIGNITY

This chapter offers a menu of gentle and rough, silly and serious, and sneaky and in-your-face moves for reducing and stopping abuse — and to send jerks packing. It contrasts with the earlier chapters that focus on changing *yourself* rather than your tormentors. I've encouraged you to fight, but not to be an idiot about it. The accompanying list highlights seven techniques that are especially prone to fail and backfire — where *strong caution and vigilance are required before and during use.*

THE WRONG WAY TO FIGHT ASSHOLES
Seven Techniques That Are Prone to Fail and Backfire

1. **Do the first thing that comes to mind, RIGHT NOW.** You encounter assholes in high-stakes and complex situations, where fear and anger can cloud your judgment. Your immediate gut instinct is probably wrong. Slow down, cool off, and talk to wise people about whether and how to fight.

2. **Use direct and aggressive confrontation with a powerful tormentor — even though you lack documentation or allies.** If you love playing the martyr or take masochistic pleasure from being abused, this approach may work for you. But if you want to change, weaken, or drive out the jerks, it usually won't work.

3. **Call an asshole an asshole.** This might work with someone you know and trust, and if done in private. But be forewarned: It usually just provokes more hostility. It's especially dangerous if it embarrasses your tormentor — and using the A-word may be an asshole move on your part.

4. **Exact vindictive, anonymous, and useless revenge.** People who lack the power or courage to confront assholes sometimes resort to anonymous and mean forms of "payback" — petty crimes like letting the air out of their tires. It may help you feel better (or worse). But in the end, it won't alter the jerks' behavior (unless they catch you and exact revenge).

5. **Find a scapegoat.** This happens when you are surrounded with assholes and have enough influence to take down one or two powerless culprits. You blame them for the rampant abuse. They are punished or expelled. You may claim the bad apples are gone, but the truth is, you haven't repaired the system. In fact, throwing a few weak jerks under the bus may actually help your cruel cronies strengthen their grip.

6. **Catch the disease to please.** This is an affliction where the creeps in question are impervious to your love bombing and ass-kissing, or worse yet, take it as a sign that you enjoy their abuse and want more. But you can't help yourself. You keep fawning over and flattering them.

7. **Ask crooked people and systems for help.** Beware of people in HR, legal, senior management, or law enforcement with big incentives to protect the assholes in power and none to fight for you. Gretchen Carlson at Fox News provides a cautionary tale. *New York* magazine reported in September 2016 that when she complained to her supervisor about condescending cohost Steve Doocy, Chairman Roger Ailes got wind of it and told Carlson that she was "a man hater" and a "killer" who "needed to get along with the boys."

That's enough handwringing. There is an upside to fighting assholes that I haven't mentioned yet, one that harkens back to chapter 5 on "Mind Tricks That Protect Your Soul." Win, lose, or draw, when you take on people who hurt you and those you care about, you've elected to defend your dignity and pride rather than allowing them to trample all over you — that alone can make you tougher and more resilient. Researchers who study workplace bullying, aggression, and abuse haven't figured out exactly when and how it's best to fight back. Bennett Tepper, who has studied abusive supervision for some twenty years, readily admitted to me, "The evidence base is still wanting." But recent studies of "upward hostility" by Tepper and his colleagues are intriguing — it appears that employees who return fire to abusive bosses (rather than acting and feeling like passive victims) feel more in control of their fates and suffer less damage.

Tepper's team did two studies of employees who responded with varying degrees of "upward hostility" to supervisors — the first followed 169 employees and the second tracked 371 employees. These researchers asked nine questions about how often each employee "resisted supervisor's requests." The questions covered direct confrontation (e.g., "I just say 'no'" and "I refuse to perform the request"), passive-aggressive payback (e.g., "I make a half-hearted effort and then let my boss know I couldn't do it"), and a blend of emotional detachment and defiance (e.g., "I ignore my supervisor" and "I disregard what my supervisor says").

The protective powers of such "upward hostility" seem striking: abused employees who fought back harder were less prone to see themselves as victims, more satisfied with their jobs and careers, less distressed, and more committed to their organizations. Tepper and his colleagues believe that employees who wrangle with and resist abusive supervisors fare better because it signals to themselves and to others that they are strong and determined to defend their dignity. They refuse to remain passive, silent, and vulnerable even though their bosses ridicule them, tell them they are stupid, and blame them unfairly.

The implication is that, while you still need to be careful about picking your battles, the rewards for fighting back may include more than reforming, repelling, defeating, and expelling the assholes that hound you. Doing so may bolster your dignity, pride, and sense of control over your fate and help you avoid feeling like a powerless victim — even if you don't win the war.

7 Be Part of the Solution, Not the Problem

THE ASSHOLE SURVIVAL GUIDE is devoted to strategies that help people escape, endure, battle, and bring down others who treat them like dirt. A simple idea runs through and glues together the stories, studies, and advice here: although we humans sometimes express it in strange ways, we all want a life where we encounter and are damaged by as few assholes as possible, we want the same thing for those we care about, and we don't want to behave like or be known as assholes. As one reader wrote me, "No one ever says, when they are on their deathbed, 'I wish I had been meaner.'"

The upshot is that the no asshole rule is a personal philosophy that shapes how you view life, the actions you take, and how you judge yourself—it's not just for teams and organizations. And it isn't just something to talk about; it means taking concrete steps. If you want to be part of the solution rather than part of the problem, it's useful to keep seven lessons in mind about what it means to live this philosophy despite the hubbub and hassles of everyday life, and our all-too-human flaws and biases.

1. Follow the da Vinci rule. Anthony Bourdain, the chef who became famous for his tell-all book *Kitchen Confidential,* and now stars in edgy food and travel TV shows, defines his success by the question "Do I like the people I am dealing with?" As he told an *Inc.* writer in 2016, "I live in business by something I call the no-asshole rule. It's an important one. I actually like everybody I do business with." Bourdain describes what living by the rule looks like:

> *We went to this one meeting in L.A. and a guy offered us a TV show and a deal that would have made us all Bond villain-wealthy. Like, helipad wealthy. The meeting went fantastically well, and we were standing there in the parking lot afterward and looked at each other, and I said, "If the phone rings at 11 p.m., do you want it to be that asshole?" And we were all like, "No way!"*

This philosophy means that when you've entered a den of assholes, you do everything possible to get out as fast as you can — or, better yet, to figure out how to avoid that lair in the first place. I call this the "da Vinci rule." As Leonardo da Vinci put it, "It is easier to resist at the beginning than at the end." That's exactly what Bourdain did. It's sound social psychology because, as I wrote in *The No Asshole Rule*, "The more time and effort that people put into anything — no matter how useless, dysfunctional, or downright stupid it might be — the harder it is for them to walk away, be it a bad investment, a destructive relationship, an exploitive job, or a workplace filled with browbeaters, bullies, and bastards."

2. Protect others, not just yourself.   As Wharton professor Adam Grant shows, the most civilized, constructive, and successful people are givers, not just takers. Just as you need others to tell you the truth about when you've been a jerk and also to shield you from demeaning people, it's smart to return their favors. It's easier to protect others, of course, when you have the authority to enforce no asshole rules. Recall Chairman Paul Purcell's warning to job candidates at Baird that he fires assholes. And remember how my Stanford colleague Perry Klebahn removes overbearing jerks from teams and puts all the bad apples in the same barrel.

You can also use your influence to install practices that nudge people to be civilized. Georgetown professor Christine Porath describes how the Louisiana-based Ochsner Health System has trained more than eleven thousand physicians, nurses, managers, and administrators the "Ochsner 10/5 Way." Employees are expected to smile at and make eye contact with any patient or employee who is within ten feet of them and to say hello to anyone who is within five feet. Porath reports that overall civility has improved, patient satisfaction is on the rise, and so are patient referrals.

Even if you aren't a top dog, you can band together with others at work to create safe havens where colleagues who are at risk of being abused can go for protection and support. A hospital administrator wrote me about how she and her colleagues protected newcomers from the wrath of the numerous jerks who roamed the halls of her hospital. I admired their reverse "asshole early warning system":

We also found staff who do NOT tend to be assholes and identified them with a small sticker on their ID badge. New staff and med students are told to use these people as resources. They are staff who have agreed to be willing to help and answer questions, and are easily identified. This has helped remove the hesitation that one has when you are new and don't know who to go to with a question (and risk getting your head bitten off).

Living this philosophy also means that when you are stuck with jerks who you can't escape from or who you can't reform, you will take on the responsibility for not catching their disease and infecting others. Even if you can't protect yourself, you will find ways to break the cycle of abuse so that future generations will be spared. A prestigious surgeon wrote me about how — when he was a surgical resident more than twenty years ago at an elite Ivy League medical school — he witnessed "episodes of unbelievable mental cruelty on a daily basis" by the senior or attending surgeons who trained him. He and his abused peers performed a little ritual that now, looking back, they believe helped them avoid becoming assholes like their mentors:

> As residents, we met every Friday for a few beers at a local bar after another arduous workweek. We kept a leather-bound journal book. The highlight of the happy hour was nominating and electing the "Attending Asshole of the Week" or "AAOTW." Each aggrieved individual would recount their episode with an attending that would merit their nomination as the "Asshole of the Week." The group voted and the "winner's" name was entered into the journal book. A brief synopsis of the "asshole incident" was also placed in the journal.

The surgeon argued this ritual wasn't just a "bitch session." "We learned how destructive asshole behavior was in our specialty," he wrote. "We vowed not to imitate the pathological behavior we encountered daily." Now, some twenty years later, those former residents all hold prestigious positions; many are program chairs and department chairs. He added, "I am proud to say that everybody who was a part of that Friday group runs their training programs with an unwritten 'no asshole' rule."

3. Use the "Benjamin Franklin effect" to turn assholes into "friends."
Recall the mantra that ends chapter 1: *"Be slow to label others as assholes, be quick to label yourself as one."* It is easy to conclude that you are dealing with a certified asshole after an encounter or two with someone who insults you, dismisses you, or treats you as if you were invisible. After all, bad behavior is more upsetting and more memorable than good behavior, and once you start suspecting that somebody is a jerk, you may focus on just their bad behavior. And if you are unkind in response, it can provoke a cycle of hostility where both of you act like jerks — so your original assumption about that other person becomes a self-fulfilling prophecy.

In particular, it's easy to leap to such conclusions about people with gruff exteriors (but who are good underneath). In chapter 5, I suggested that a useful reframing strategy was "develop sympathy for the devil," to tell yourself that a known asshole is a "porcupine with a heart of gold" or has "a bad user interface but a good operating system" in nerdspeak. Such attributions sometimes turn out to be accurate descriptions, not just mind tricks for coping with a bully or backstabber. So before you label someone as an asshole, it's helpful to you, the suspected jerk, and those around you to consider alternative explanations.

Beyond jumping to conclusions, when people do treat you like dirt, you might be able to reverse the situation by using love bombing, as we saw in chapter 6. Respond to their nastiness with relentless civility and warmth, and see if they treat you better — as my daughter Claire did to reform the grumpy cook at that restaurant she worked at in Boston. Better yet, combine your warmth and flattery with requests that they do a small favor or two FOR YOU. This strategy is akin to what author David McRaney calls "the Benjamin Franklin effect," which is based on experiments that show we come to like people that we do nice things for and to dislike people that we treat unkindly.

In *You Are Now Less Dumb*, McRaney describes how, when Franklin was a young man struggling to overcome his modest means and lack of formal education, a wealthy and educated peer (whom he doesn't name in his writings) gave a long speech attacking Franklin's actions and motives. Franklin was furious. But he didn't return the anger. Instead, McRaney explained how Franklin transformed "his hater into a fan":

> *Franklin's reputation as a book collector and library founder gave him a standing as a man of discerning literary tastes, so Franklin sent a letter to the hater asking if he could borrow a specific selection from his library, one that was a "very scarce and curious book." The rival, flattered, sent it right away. Franklin sent it back a week later with a thank-you note. Mission accomplished. The next time the legislature met, the man approached Franklin and spoke to him in person for the first time. Franklin said the man "ever after manifested a readiness to serve me on all occasions, so that we became great friends, and our friendship continued to his death."*

I first read about this Benjamin Franklin effect on Maria Popova's wonderful *Brain Pickings* website. Popova's interpretation of why this ploy works helps explain why you see others as assholes, why they see you as one, and how to reverse the associated hostile sentiments and acts: "This is what happened to Franklin's nemesis: He observed himself performing an act of kindness toward Franklin, which he explained to himself by constructing the most plausible story — that he did so willfully, because he liked Franklin after all."

It may sound daft. But no matter how much disdain someone feels and expresses to you, if you can entice them to offer a bit of kindness to you, they may change their tune. This lesson cuts both ways: if you want to reduce the abuse that you heap on others, start to do favors for your targets, say something kind to them, and do something nice for them behind their backs. Such strategies create uncomfortable cognitive dissonance — when people change their behavior, their judgments and feelings usually fall into line so they can justify their actions to themselves and others. That's why McRaney advises, "Above all, remember the more harm you cause, the more hate you feel. The more kindness you express, the more you come to love those you help."

4. Take a look in the mirror — are you part of the problem?   "Every group has an asshole. If you look around and don't see one, that means it is you." I think I heard that joke from comedian Craig Ferguson, the former host of *The Late Late Show* on CBS. It provides a nice reminder that if you are a jerk, sometimes the person least likely to realize it is you. And if you feel besieged by assholes, even if you are part (or all) of the problem, it won't be easy for you to admit it to yourself or anybody else. That's why, as reported at the end of chapter 1, over 50% of Americans say they have experienced or witnessed persistent bullying, but less than 1% admit to doing it — those numbers don't add up; a lot of jerks out there aren't confessing their sins.

Alas, we human beings have a penchant for denial and delusion. We are often clueless about our flaws, and when we do admit our shortcomings, we underestimate their severity and negative impact.

I've discussed the curse of overconfidence and how Nobel Prize winner Daniel Kahneman believes it is the most destructive of human biases. We tend to see ourselves through rose-colored glasses. Others who know us (even slightly) are often much better judges of our strengths and (especially) weaknesses. Dozens of studies conducted and inspired by psychologists David Dunning and Justin Kruger show that poor performers are especially prone to delusions: they overestimate their talents, including logical reasoning, grammar, humor, debating, interviewing, management, and emotional skills. In fact, the weaker their skills, including interpersonal skills, the more that people tend to exaggerate them in their own minds.

If you think of yourself as a civilized person but seem to run into assholes everywhere that you go, look in the mirror — you could be staring at the culprit. Remember, treating others like dirt goads people to bully you back. As we've seen, research on abusive supervision and workplace aggression shows that returning fire provokes targets. Consider one of the weirdest encounters that I had after publishing *The No Asshole Rule*. I met a prestigious attorney at a Stanford entrepreneurship conference who told me that he liked the book. He bragged about how he lived the rule and took pride in treating everyone with full respect — even though he dealt with numerous rude and selfish people every day.

I was astonished to hear all of this because, although I didn't tell him, he was the same attorney described in that book who had offered my wife Marina a job; she turned it down after one of his former associates told Marina that he was a flaming asshole (and backed up his claim with multiple stories). Sure enough, as reported in *The No Asshole Rule*, when the attorney learned that Marina had declined the job, he called her "to berate and criticize her and to pressure her to reveal the insider who had outed him." Her response was "Your behavior on this call confirms the reasons behind this decision." That attorney didn't connect me to Marina because years had passed since the incident and Marina and I have different last names. But he seems to be the poster child for every clueless asshole who doesn't realize how badly he treats people (or sees himself as so insightful and brilliant that his — and only his — demeaning moves ought to be allowed) and travels through life without realizing that people are throwing back the same shit that he throws at them.

We human beings are prone to developing distorted and overly positive self-images — and to deny, disregard, or never notice negative information about ourselves. That means that, for most of us, coming to grips with when we act like jerks or encouraging others to do so requires overcoming some mighty potent predilections. As Columbia University psychologist Heidi Grant Halvorson documents in *No One Understands You and What to Do About It,* the key to self-awareness isn't found inside our heads; it's in discovering and accepting how *others* see us — even when it hurts. Halvorson shows that the bigger the gap between how we see ourselves and how others see us, the worse our relationships with them tend to be. So there is a big payoff to coming to grips with how others perceive us. The people in our lives tend to agree with each other about how we've acted in the past and probably will act in the future — their judgments are usually far more accurate than our own self-assessments. The takeaway is, if you want to know if someone is an asshole, they are the worst person to ask.

But the path to self-awareness is easy to describe and hard to follow: You need people who know you and who won't sugarcoat the truth, and to seek and accept candid feedback from them. When they give you bad news, thank them, don't argue, try not to look angry or devastated, and — this is tough if you have narcissistic tendencies — stifle any thoughts that they've somehow betrayed you, you are going to shun them, or even worse, you're going to exact revenge.

Here is how a master truth-teller practiced this craft on me. Peter Glynn was my department chair at Stanford for five years. Peter is a modest and unselfish Canadian with strong opinions about civility and justice. I once had a student who made many irrelevant comments in class and who also generated numerous complaints from fellow students about his poor work and destructive attitude. After this student handed in a bad paper, I wrote him a blistering email that went far beyond specific critiques of the work: I questioned his character and implied he was lazy and clueless. The student (rightfully) forwarded my email to Peter, who called me into his office, told me that no faculty member should ever treat any student that way, and demanded that I apologize to the student at once. Of course, Peter was right. I apologized profusely to the student and I thanked Peter for calling me out on my cruel email. That conversation with Peter stung. That is what living the no asshole rule looks and feels like — the truth hurts, but things are even worse when people are unwilling or unable to tell or hear it.

My Stanford colleague Huggy Rao argues that if you look at many successful people, they have a spouse or partner who informs them when they have acted like an asshole or an idiot — even when other friends, colleagues, and followers are afraid to deliver them the bad news. Recall the letter that Prime Minister Winston Churchill's wife Clementine wrote him in 1940, during the darkest days of World War II for Britain. Clementine didn't pull any punches: "I must confess that I have noticed a deterioration in your manner; & you are not so kind as you used to be."

Huggy speculates further that powerful people with teenage children are less prone to arrogance and delusions of grandeur because, no matter how much their underlings and fans fawn over and flatter them, they've got young people at home who don't hesitate to point out their flaws and foibles day after day. Researchers haven't tested this hypothesis; but when I present it to leaders as a possible antidote to hubris, they laugh, nod, and tell me stories about how their own children bring them back to earth.

You can reduce your risk of treating others poorly by seeking out and listening to trusted truth-tellers and reflecting about your past behavior to identify circumstances that bring out the worst in you. Check out the attached list of a dozen risk factors that researchers have identified — these are common "Achilles' heels" that cause people to act like or to be seen by others as rude, overly aggressive, abusive, and bullying — and figure out which ones are especially likely to cause your inner jerk to rear its ugly head.

WHAT IS YOUR ACHILLES' HEEL?
Factors That Encourage People to Act Like and to Be Viewed as Assholes

1. You are around a lot of assholes.
2. You wield power over others — especially if you once had little power.
3. You are at the top of the pecking order, and are a very competitive person who feels threatened by your star underlings.
4. You are rich.

5. You are seen as a "cold" person.
6. You work much harder and sacrifice more than others — and often let everyone know about your martyrdom.
7. You are a "Rule Nazi," a stickler who follows every rule precisely and insists that others do as well.
8. You don't get enough sleep.
9. You have too much to do, too much to think about, and always seem to be in a hurry.
10. You feel a constant urge to look at your smartphone, which you can't resist even when you know you should exercise self-control.
11. You are a man and have a woman for a boss. Perhaps you are an exception, but researchers found that men tend to feel more threatened by female than male bosses.
12. You tend to be cynical and negative about most things (some people are like that).

Three risks are especially prevalent and potent. I've already raised the first. If you are around assholes, you are likely to catch the disease because such bad behavior is so contagious. Recall the research in chapter 4 by Trevor Foulk and his colleagues that showed how rude behavior spreads like a common cold. They tracked research subjects who engaged in eleven simulated negotiations over a seven-week period, and subjects who encountered even one rude partner were prone to become "carriers" and to be rude during their next negotiation (with a different partner). Imagine how powerful such effects are when you are surrounded with jerks every day, all day long. That's why it is so risky to hang out with or work with assholes; you might vow to resist infection or to change how those around you behave. But when it is you versus *a lot* of assholes, odds are *you* are going to become more like them — not the other way around. We humans automatically and mindlessly start mimicking the facial expressions, tone, and language that surrounds us. And, if you are surrounded with jerks, it's often difficult to survive without returning their fire.

As we've seen, there are some people (especially those with Machiavellian personalities) who don't understand anything else. They see your kindness and cooperation as a sign of weakness, rather than as a favor that ought to be returned. There are also hints from that recent research by Bennett Tepper that employees who push back against abusive supervisors — including by openly refusing their orders and requests — enjoy better mental health.

In particular, if you are in a *Lord of the Flies* situation, where cruelty, backstabbing, and selfishness are everywhere, a protective layer of nastiness may be the only way you can survive the onslaught. A project manager wrote me how, at his former place of employment, "jerks begot jerks" and senior management's most favored underlings "were as snide and arrogant as them, lashing out at more junior employees and using them as sacrifices for their personal agendas." The manager admitted, "It brought out the asshole in me," and he was "frequently irate, overly forceful, and overbearing" because "it seemed to be the only way to get things done." Of course, battling with assholes day after day exacts a terrible toll (even if you act like one too). The "bad dreams, stress, and frustration" drove this manager to quit and move to a small company "with a strict no asshole policy," and his friends and family have noticed that he's become "much nicer, calmer, and more confident."

Wielding power over others is the second big risk that you will eventually start treating others like dirt. Professor Dacher Keltner from the University of California at Berkeley has devoted more than twenty years to studying the effects of wielding power over others and simply feeling powerful; the findings aren't pretty. Regardless of how kind, cooperative, and empathetic you've acted in the past, Keltner and other psychologists show that power can cause you to have less empathy for others, to exploit them more, to focus more on your own needs and less on the needs of others, to be rude and disrespectful, and to act like the rules don't apply to you.

To give you a taste, Keltner reports that wealthy people are more prone to such unflattering tendencies because, after all, being rich means that you have high social status, the ability to influence others, and to get more of what you want — all elements of power. In one study, Keltner's students observed how drivers in Berkeley behaved at a busy four-way stop that had heavy automobile and pedestrian traffic. These researchers found that drivers in the least expensive cars (e.g., an old Dodge Colt) cut in front of other drivers at the intersection less than 10% of the time and always stopped for pedestrians. In contrast, those drivers in the most expensive cars (e.g., a new Mercedes-Benz) cut in front of other drivers about 30% of the time and failed to stop for pedestrians nearly 50% of the time.

If you want to avoid power poisoning, having truth-tellers in your life who bring you down a notch is essential, as we saw with Winston Churchill's wife Clementine and with my department chair Peter Glynn. Other antidotes include practicing humility, giving credit to less powerful people, deferring to people who are less prestigious or wealthy than you, doing them favors, and expressing gratitude. The idea is to enable others to feel more powerful and esteemed. And use the Benjamin Franklin effect — try to behave in ways that help you see yourself as not being "above" fellow human beings — and as somebody who consciously thinks about what others feel and want (rather than just about yourself).

Tim Brown, the CEO of the renowned innovation firm IDEO, demonstrates how this is done (full disclosure: I am an IDEO fellow and sometimes work with their clients). As first described on my *Work Matters* blog in 2010, I went to the IDEO office in Palo Alto for a visit and walked up to the floor where many of the senior leaders in the firm worked. When I turned the corner, there was Tim Brown, sitting in the front where a receptionist would be in most workplaces. There was no gatekeeper to keep either colleagues or random visitors like myself from walking up and interrupting him. I assumed that this was a mistake because, the last time I had visited, Tim had a private office on that floor. I asked him why he wasn't in his office. Tim explained he had abandoned the office and moved to a spot that made him "the most public person on the floor."

Tim told me that most IDEO senior leaders had moved out of their offices too — which meant that when a private conversation was called for, there were now many small conference rooms available (i.e., their old offices). He added that when he became the CEO in 2005, he was given his own office for the first time in his long career at the company — which he found "vaguely embarrassing and frustrating." After a while, he and others tried a different approach, where they were out in the open and had more casual exchanges and there were fewer barriers. Tim emphasized that his job was "to get to know the people and how they work" and, he said, "I can't learn much sitting in a private office."

The lesson from Tim's story isn't that every senior executive ought to move out of their office — open offices have a host of disadvantages, especially when organizations are filled with jerks (it's harder to hide from assholes when there are no walls), don't discourage loud talk and interruptions, and have few places where people can go for meetings and private conversations. Rather, the lesson is that finding ways to reduce the "power distance" between you and others not only decreases their stress but also increases their contributions; it also changes how you see yourself in ways that can prevent you from acting like a selfish bully.

Efforts to decrease unnecessary power differences are also evident in the little things that powerful people say to others. A reader wrote me with a charming illustration. It happened way back in 1971, when she was an extra in a movie directed by the late Peter Ustinov, and it still warms her heart:

> *I happened to have a chance to speak with him during the day, but he asked me first "who are you?" (not just a little intimidating) and I replied "oh, nobody, I'm just an extra." His mostly lovely response to me was "Young woman! Without extras and audiences there is no movie!" I think those were the neatest words I ever heard from a leader and I've kept a calligraphy of it on my wall ever since.*

Overload is the third big risk. Being in a rush, having too much to do, and having too many distractions can turn even the most civilized person into a jerk. Christine Porath's surveys of hundreds of employees from diverse industries found that over 50% admit that they've engaged in uncivilized behavior at work at times — these are slights such as failing to say "please" and "thank you," sending emails or texts during meetings, and belittling others. As she wrote in the *New York Times* in 2015, "Over half of them claim it is because they are overloaded, and more than 40 percent say they have no time to be nice." When I talk to managers and executives about overload, meetings are one of the primary culprits that they identify. If you want shorter meetings that will be just as effective, just try standing up instead of sitting down. One experiment found that groups that stood up in meetings took 34% less time to make a decision compared to groups where people sat down, and the quality of their decisions did not suffer.

It's even better to get rid of meetings altogether. The "Armeetingeddon" purge at Dropbox in 2013 illustrates how to accomplish this feat — I learned about it after one of my favorite students, Rebecca Hinds, went to work at Dropbox and we investigated the story further. As Rebecca and I reported in *Inc.,* this fast-growing file-sharing and storage company was plagued with overload — people were working crazy hours, were grumpy and sleep deprived, and kept missing deadlines — it was a vicious cycle. Part of the problem was that people were spending more and more time in meetings — and the number of people at each meeting had ballooned. So senior executives instructed IT staffers to go into each employee's online calendar and delete all upcoming meetings (except ones with customers). IT also made it impossible to enter any meetings in these calendars for two weeks.

This purge was announced with the battle cry "Armeetingeddon has landed" in the subject line of an email sent to Dropbox employees. This "meeting subtraction" forced employees to think about the overload they inflicted on themselves and others. As they manually reentered each upcoming meeting in their calendar, they were asked to consider if they needed it and whether it could happen less often, be shorter, or involve fewer people. Dropbox also introduced related guidelines to cut overload, including a suggested cap of three to five people per meeting and encouragement to walk out of any meeting where you were not adding or learning enough to justify your presence there.

Multitasking, checking emails, and using smartphones probably contribute to overload even more than unnecessary meetings for most of us. These modern necessities — and addictions — can cause us to be curt, treat others as if they were invisible, and devote too little attention to our colleagues, friends, and family, and they entice us to devote too much attention to the irresistible temptations of Facebook, Twitter, Snapchat, Instagram, email, and the like. In April 2016, the *ScienceDaily* website reported that the Civility in America survey of 1,005 adults had found that almost all Americans (93%) said that civility was a problem in the United States and over 50% named the Internet and social media as a primary cause (just after rude politicians).

When it comes to overcoming such electronic temptations, each of us needs to exercise self-control; it helps to nudge each other to turn off our phones and put them away. Imposing rules on yourself — and others if possible — can be helpful for avoiding "smartphone attention deficit disorder." When Chris Fry was head of engineering at Twitter in 2014, he was disturbed that members of his senior team were looking at their smartphones so much that it undermined communication and civility during meetings. Chris, who also has a PhD in cognitive psychology, is well versed in research that shows how smartphones can turn us into dumb creatures who perform our work less well and devote less attention to other's ideas and feelings. So Chris implemented a policy where team members were required to give their phones to his executive assistant for safekeeping during meetings. One of his team members even sent out a tweet that said,

"@chfry rule cell phones must be deposited with @rjsanjose prior to the start of the meeting" and included a picture of six phones stashed on a table.

5. Apologize when you've behaved like an asshole — but only if you really mean it and then do it right.   Living the no asshole rule sometimes means that when you've treated others like dirt, you feel obliged to apologize. A well-crafted apology can help reduce your target's pain, repair your relationship with them and bystanders you've offended, improve your reputation, and provoke some soul-searching that enables you to learn from your transgressions. Here's how to do it.

In June 2016, film director John Carney made headlines and was ravaged on social media for belittling actress Keira Knightley, one of the stars of his 2014 film *Begin Again*. Carney accused Knightley of having an entourage that followed her everywhere, making it "very hard to get any real work done." He also said she couldn't sing, and he complained, "I'll never make a film with supermodels again." A few days later, as *Salon*'s website reported, Carney sent out a tweet that said, "From a director who feels like a complete idiot" and included a pitch-perfect apology:

> *I said a number of things about Keira which were petty, mean and hurtful. I'm ashamed of myself that I could say such things and I've been trying to account for what they say about me. In trying to pick holes in my own work, I ended up blaming someone else. That's not only bad directing, that's shoddy behaviour, that I am not proud of. It's arrogant and disrespectful. Keira was nothing but professional and dedicated during the*

film and she contributed hugely to its success. I wrote to Keira
personally to apologise, but I wanted to publicly, and unreserv-
edly apologise to her fans and friends and anyone else who I
have offended. It's not something that I could ever justify, and
will never repeat.

The sincerity and lack of qualification in this apology is obvious. But it's instructive to use research on the differences between
good and bad apologies to understand the nuances. Following studies by Ohio State University's Roy Lewicki and his colleagues, Carney's apology contains the most important element of a good and
effective apology: he acknowledges that he is clearly at fault, it is
a mistake, and he accepts full responsibility and does so without a
hint of waffling. Carney doesn't make the classic error of apologizing for *her* feelings, of saying something lame like "I am sorry if
what I said made you feel bad." He owns his actions by stating that
his words were "petty, mean and hurtful." It also contains the second
most important element of a good apology identified in Lewicki's
studies: Carney did what he could to make repairs — he apologized
to her privately first, then in this public forum, and then praised her
performance.

Carney adds three more useful twists that, according to the research, are helpful but less crucial elements of a good apology: he
expresses regret, tries to explain why it happened (because of his
own insecurity about his work), and repents and commits to personal change by asserting it is something he "will never repeat." His
apology also lacks something that Lewicki's team found was the least
important part of a good apology (although not something that is
necessarily destructive): he doesn't ask for forgiveness — I suspect

that was something Carney hoped for but thought it best not to ask for, as that was Keira's choice and not something he should ask for or insist upon.

Despite the virtues of apologies, two caveats are in order. First, if you feel as if someone has treated you like dirt, demanding that they apologize to you rarely works. Given that so many assholes are clueless, they may respond that YOU are the one who should apologize (and may even be right). And even if you browbeat them so much that they give in and do apologize, it's unlikely to be sincere.

Second, if you find yourself apologizing again and again for being an asshole, it's time to stop. It's probably a sign that you are using apologies as a substitute for learning and toning down your act. And the impact on your victims will diminish as they tire of the cycle of abuse, apology, followed by more abuse, and then more apologies. That's what happened to the PhD student that I wrote about in chapter 4 who used "the rhythm method" to decrease the frequency of encounters with her abusive dissertation advisor. It took the student a while to realize how destructive her advisor was because, after a string of abusive emails, calls, and conversations, the advisor would then go through a "hearts and flowers" stage — appear remorseful, make promises to behave better, and appeal to her forgiving nature. She told me that "he would sometimes send me personalized poetry via email about our 'great' relationship, leave touching songs on my voicemail, compliment me, and even cry tears in meetings and say that he was afraid I would leave him to work with someone else." Then the advisor soon returned to his abusive ways. Eventually, the student saw through the "hearts and flowers" nonsense and "learned to stop responding entirely to anything unprofessional." She concluded that this advisor, whether he realized it or not, was using this ploy to weaken the defenses that she would need after he returned to his usual demeaning and disrespectful ways.

6. Are you a toxic enabler?   You may not treat people like dirt, but you may fuel asshole problems by serving as a toxic enabler for one or more bullies — whether you realize it or not. Toxic enablers make it easier for jerks to do their dirty deeds and to avoid suffering the negative consequences of their destructive behavior. A hallmark of "successful" assholes is that they recruit, entice, or bribe toxic enablers to clean up the messes they leave behind — much like the cleanup crew that picks up the trash and poop after the circus parades through a town.

Peter Frost, in *Toxic Emotions at Work,* describes these characters as part of a "good cop/bad cop configuration," which often begins when the enabler or "handler" realizes that the pain inflicted by an abusive boss needs to be managed and the boss realizes that "things go more smoothly" when the enabler does "people work" to soften the blows and pick up the pieces after his or her emotional storms. Frost describes a toxic senior executive who brought the same "chief lieutenant" with him to a series of roles over a fifteen-year stretch. After meetings where the boss had attacked people with angry tirades, for example, the enabler "would walk from office to office, explaining the boss's 'real' opinions and assuring people he was not as angry as he seemed." The most destructive enablers also prevent toxic tormentors from facing their ugly selves by assuring them that their behavior is understandable or acceptable, that their victims deserved it, or perhaps assuring them that while they did blow it this time, that's not who they "really" are (even if they are all asshole all the time).

As Frost implies, if you play such a role, you are part of the problem rather than the solution. Although skilled "handlers" provide temporary relief for victims and abusers, they can "enable people and organizational systems to continue generating pain, year after year, with no corrective consequences, they in effect 'cover up' the sources of pain — to everyone's detriment." I talked with the former second in command of a large Silicon Valley company who admitted that he spent nearly a decade cooling out and calming down the legions of upset people who had been bruised by his infamously temperamental, vindictive, and impatient CEO. It took him years to realize that, rather than serving as an antidote to the CEO's poison, he was making things worse.

If you are a boss, you are also a toxic enabler if you make excuses for destructive underlings and instruct their damaged colleagues to toughen up — rather than doing your job and dealing with the culprits' bad behavior. For example, I heard from a reader who had been moved next to a "foul mouthed, loud, nosey, bossy, opinionated, illiterate, judgmental, arrogant, and just plain nasty" teammate. He wrote, "Within 30 days of this exposure, I was in the hospital diagnosed with a duodenal ulcer." To prove how loud his tormentor was, the reader bought a decibel meter and measured her volume. The email he sent me included "a photo of the meter showing a level of 44.1 decibels when she is NOT in the office," "a photo showing a machine shop during the process of cutting a keyway in a steel hub at 72.3 decibels," and a picture taken when his coworker was "on the phone giving someone hell at 85.8 decibels."

When this beleaguered reader went to his boss to complain and threaten to quit, he was told "to just let her BS go in one ear and out the other." The reader was the fourth person on the team to get the same advice from their boss about dealing with this abusive loudmouth — and they each concluded that neither their boss nor anyone else in the company had the courage to discipline, move, or fire their horrible colleague. That spineless boss was a classic toxic enabler. If you are in management and respond to complaints and evidence about an abusive employee by telling their victims to suck it up, and you don't do a thing to change or remove the offender, you are indeed part of the problem rather than the solution.

7. Do a little time travel.   In chapter 5, I described how the human capacity for "mental time travel" can ease the pain caused by a current asshole — how it helps to tell yourself that what feels so awful now will be no big deal after it ends and you look back on it later. This same superpower can be harnessed to help you live the no asshole rule. As the reader quoted at the outset of this chapter said, "No one ever says, when they are on their deathbed, 'I wish I had been meaner.'" That saying reminds me of a former FBI agent who wrote me that he is "a recovering asshole" and how, just like a recovering alcoholic, it's something that he needs to fight "one day at a time." This guy was ashamed of his past bad behavior. Later, when he looks back on his life, he wants to feel proud of how he treated others after his recovery commenced — and that framing of his life helps him to treat the people around him in more civilized ways day after day.

This brand of imaginary time travel is among my favorite research-based means for bringing out the best and stifling the worst in people. It entails deciding what to do *today* based on how you want to feel when you look back from the *future*. When it comes to living the no asshole rule, this means that (much like that former FBI agent), as you move through each day, it's useful to pretend that it's a day, a week, a month, or a year later — and that you feel proud of how you have responded to and treated others. Think about the nuances of what you must have done. What did you do to protect yourself from the demeaning people that you faced? How did you quell their hostility and fight back? What actions did you do to treat others with dignity and respect?

So take a look back from your imaginary future. It can help you do the right thing right now.

OF PLANS AND PORCUPINES

A thought before we go: *it's on you* AND *you are not alone.*

These two intertwined ideas provide a nice compact summary of how to deal with any given asshole problem. They also reveal much about why such problems are an inevitable part of the human condition — and how we can avoid driving each other crazy despite all the pressures and temptations to do so.

The Asshole Survival Guide emphasizes that if you feel oppressed, disrespected, demeaned, or de-energized by others, it's on you to create, implement, and keep refining your plan. The studies, stories, and techniques here provide fodder for crafting your custom survival strategy (after all, there are no surefire, one-size-fits-all solutions). And by realizing you are not alone, by turning to people ranging from fellow targets to friends and to your family for support and wisdom, you bolster your chances of constructing better plans, traveling through difficult days with dignity and grace, and emerging from it all as a stronger person.

"It's on me" and "I am not alone" also reflect the opposing forces that create asshole problems in the first place. We are each responsible for taking care of ourselves. At the same time, we need other people for emotional and physical sustenance, and others need sustenance from us. Along the way, sometimes we ask for too much from them, they ask for too much from us, and we bruise each other's spirit. Our collective challenge is to get what we need from each other without hurting each other.

Harvard University biologist Edward O. Wilson relates a charming German fable from his colleague Paul Leyhausen that captures the essence of these tensions and how people can band together to deal with them. It's about a group of porcupines that huddled for warmth one freezing night. But as they huddled, they poked each other with their spines. So they moved apart and then got too cold. Leyhausen concludes, "After shuffling repeatedly in and out, they eventually found a distance at which they could still be comfortably warm without getting pricked. This distance they henceforth called decency and good manners."

Those porcupines are a lot like people. If we each took it upon ourselves to share as much warmth with others as possible without injuring them or ourselves, there would be more places infused with decency and good manners, and far fewer assholes, on this planet.

Your Stories and Ideas

Dear Reader,

As you've seen throughout *The Asshole Survival Guide*, I've learned a great deal from people who have sent me their stories and advice. Let's keep it going. If you would like to send me an email about your experiences with assholes, what you've learned about escaping, enduring, or defeating them, or anything else related to dealing with demeaning and disrespectful people, please send it to nomorejerks@gmail.com. I read every email and do my best to answer each one. Please note that, by sending me your story, you are giving me permission to use it in the things that I write and say. BUT I promise not to use your name unless you give me explicit permission. I also invite you to follow, tweet to, or message me on Twitter @work_matters.

Thanks, and I look forward to learning from you.

Robert Sutton
Stanford University

Acknowledgments

DURING THE YEAR OR SO that I devoted my days to writing this book, when people asked what I was doing, I often joked, "I am trying to type my way out of solitary confinement in my garage." That answer was both true and false. It was true because I wrote *The Asshole Survival Guide* in the little study in my garage, and the only way to escape was to finish the thing. As any author can tell you, long stretches of solo concentration are required to finish any book. But that joke is misleading because it implies that this book was a solo effort. It would have been impossible to write it without so much help (and tolerance for my many quirks) from so many talented, patient, and altruistic colleagues, friends, and family.

Two people played especially crucial roles. Professor Katy DeCelles from the University of Toronto visited Stanford during the 2015–2016 academic year. Katy not only gave me many ideas for the book from her research, studies conducted by other scholars, and her creativity and common sense — she encouraged me to start it and, later, finish it at junctures where my motivation had waned. The second key person is Michael Dearing, a venture capitalist and former senior executive with whom I taught innovation classes at Stanford for years. For nearly a decade now, Michael has nudged me (and sometimes badgered me) to write this book. He argued that I owed my readers much deeper advice about how to deal with assholes. And, given Michael's strong sales and marketing background, he urged me to write this book to strengthen my claim to the "hole franchise."

I thank Stanford colleagues Steve Barley, Tom Byers, Peter Glynn, Chip Heath, Pam Hinds, David Kelley, Perry Klebahn, Huggy Rao, Bernie Roth, Tina Seelig, Kathryn Segovia, Jeremy Utley, and Melissa Valentine for their varied and provocative suggestions and insights. And as always, I thank Jeff Pfeffer. As usual, he disagrees with some of my conclusions and advice, and has forced me to think more deeply about my ideas. I also appreciate the ideas and encouragement from academics and authors outside of Stanford, including Michel Anteby, Eric Barker, Laszlo Bock, Adam Grant, Julia Kirby, Dan Pink, Christine Porath, and Bennett Tepper. A small army of skilled and patient Stanford staff repeatedly saved me from myself during the past two years or so including Lori Cottle, Tim Keely, Paul Marca, Marilynn Rose, Ronie Shilo, Danielle Steussy, and especially Matt Harvey. Former Stanford students Deanna Badizadegan, Rebecca Hinds, and Joachim Bendix Lyon helped with the research for this book along the way.

I am grateful to the thousands of people who sent me emails with their "asshole stories," and told me such stories in person, on the phone, or via social media. Although I can't name most of you, your questions, suggestions, suffering, joy, and humor inspired me to write this book and shaped it in hundreds of ways. I also thank those contributors who I can name for their stories and suggestions, including IDEO's Tim Brown, Pixar's Ed Catmull, former Salesforce and Twitter executive Chris Fry, Twitter executive Steve Green, Philz Coffee CEO Jacob Jaber, the Billions Institute's Becky Margiotta (for her stories about being a West Point cadet), former Netflix executive and all-around straight-talker Patty McCord, Baird's Paul Purcell, JetBlue's Bonny Simi, and the *Wall Street Journal's* Jason Zweig.

Christy Fletcher is my persistent, wise, and supportive literary agent. Christy not only provided encouragement, advice, and skilled editing on the proposal, and sold this book to the right editor and publisher for me — she is adept at giving me candid feedback when I push an editor or publisher too hard on some minor point (and encouraging me to push back even harder at other times). I am grateful to the skilled team at Fletcher & Company, including Hillary Black, Melissa Chinchillo, Gráinne Fox, Sarah Fuentes, Veronica Goldstein, Sylvie Greenberg, and Erin McFadden for the all the ways that they steer this and my other book projects through the crazy rules, traditions, and characters in the book publishing industry.

The best part of writing this book has been working with Rick Wolff; he also edited *The No Asshole Rule* and *Good Boss, Bad Boss,* so we know each other well. Rick is a joy to work with. He is relentlessly supportive and encouraging, understands my weaknesses and how to dampen them, and is particularly adept at repairing my garbled and over-the-top text without flattening the spirit or distorting the arguments or evidence. I am delighted that Rick has joined Bruce Nichols at Houghton Mifflin Harcourt; Bruce has been equally supportive of *The Asshole Survival Guide.* And I am tickled to be reunited with Bruce too, as he did a wonderful job as my editor for *Weird Ideas That Work* back in 2001, which was my first sole-authored book. I am grateful to Rosemary McGuinness for shepherding the book through HMH's sometimes mysterious system. I thank the charming Daniel Crewe from Penguin Random House (which publishes this book in the United Kingdom) for his thoughtful comments and suggestions. And I thank Justin Gammon, Brian Moore,

Becky Saikia-Wilson, Chris Sergio, and Michaela Sullivan for their patience and persistence in developing some sixty-five prototypes of the cover design, including over thirty variations of the "Alka-Seltzer" concept that we ultimately selected.

I never thought that I would use the words "fun" and "copyediting" in the same sentence. But here it comes. I am grateful to copyeditor Kristin Vorce Duran for taking the time to understand my writing style and goals before her work began, and for communicating with me so well at the outset and along the way. Kristin was careful and skilled, and changed the book for the better in hundreds of little ways, but never trampled on my writing voice. So I am surprised, but delighted, to say that, for the first time in my life, the copyediting process was downright fun.

Finally, this book is dedicated to my three children, Eve, Claire, and Tyler. Now, as young adults, they tell me many inspiring, funny, and horrifying tales about navigating around, and sometimes battling, the difficult and oppressive people that they encounter. I love and appreciate each of you more than I can express. And I owe everything to my wife, Marina. Her patience, wisdom, candor, and nonstop love make life better every day for Eve, Claire, Tyler, and me. Marina's compassion for every person that she encounters in this life still astounds me even after all our years together.

Notes

1. EIGHT THOUSAND EMAILS

PAGE

3 *It all started:* Robert I. Sutton, *The No Asshole Rule: Building a Civilized Workplace and Surviving One That Isn't* (New York: Business Plus, 2007).

5 *follow-up questions:* This book presents accurate reflections of the emails, media reports, personal experiences, conversations, and interviews that I collected. For most emails and some observations, conversations, and experiences, I have not named the parties involved to protect the confidentiality that I promised to people who told me their stores. And in fewer than half a dozen cases, I have changed information including gender, location, and occupation to protect the identity of people who were especially concerned about revealing their names or those of their tormentors.

6 *"dudes and bros":* Tucker Max, *Assholes Finish First* (New York: Simon & Schuster, 2011).

8 *rude American health-care expert:* Arieh Riskin, Amir Erez, Trevor A. Foulk, Amir Kugelman, Ayala Gover, Irit Shoris, Kinneret S. Riskin, and Peter A. Bamberger, "The Impact of Rudeness on Medical Team Performance: A Randomized Trial," *Pediatrics* 136, no. 3 (2015): 487–495.

9 *more civilized patients:* H. G. Schmidt, Tamara van Gog, Stephanie C. E. Schuit, Kees Van den Berge, Paul L. A. Van Daele, Herman Bueving, Tim Van der Zee, Walter W. Van den Broek, Jan L.C.M. Van Saase, and Sílvia Mamede, "Do Patients' Disruptive Behaviours Influence the Accuracy of a Doctor's Diagnosis? A Randomised Experiment," *BMJ Quality & Safety* 26, no. 1 (2017): 19–23.

studies of bullied children: Shelley Hymel and Susan M. Swearer, "Four Decades of Research on School Bullying: An Introduction," *American Psychologist* 70, no. 4 (2015): 293.

Research on workplace assholes: Based on reviews including Birgit Schyns and Jan Schilling, "How Bad Are the Effects of Bad Leaders? A Meta-Analysis of Destructive Leadership and Its Outcomes," *Leadership Quarterly* 24, no. 1 (2013): 138–158; Al-Karim Samnani and Parbudyal Singh, "20 Years of Workplace Bullying Research: A Review of the Antecedents and Consequences of Bullying in the Workplace," *Aggression and Violent Behavior* 17, no. 6 (2012): 581–589.

New nurses: Peggy A. Berry, Gordon L. Gillespie, Donna Gates, and John Schafer, "Novice Nurse Productivity Following Workplace Bullying," *Journal of Nursing Scholarship* 44, no. 1 (2012): 80–87.

Service employees: Mo Wang, Songqi Liu, Hui Liao, Yaping Gong, John Kammeyer-Mueller, and Junqi Shi, "Can't Get It Out of My Mind: Employee Rumination After Customer Mistreatment and Negative Mood in the Next Morning," *Journal of Applied Psychology* 98, no. 6 (2013): 989.

10 *who observe customers abusing:* Kathryne E. Dupré, Kimberly-Anne Dawe, and Julian Barling, "Harm to Those Who Serve: Effects of Direct and Vicarious Customer-Initiated Workplace Aggression," *Journal of Interpersonal Violence* 29, no. 13 (2014): 2355–2377.

selecting or breeding abusive team leaders: Dong Liu, Hui Liao, and Raymond Loi, "The Dark Side of Leadership: A Three-Level Investigation of the Cascading Effect of Abusive Supervision on Employee Creativity," *Academy of Management Journal* 55, no. 5 (2012): 1187–1212.

$23.8 billion a year: Bennett J. Tepper, Michelle K. Duffy, Christine A. Henle, and Lisa Schurer Lambert, "Procedural Injustice, Victim Precipitation, and Abusive Supervision," *Personnel Psychology* 59, no. 1 (2006): 101–123.

deaths from heart disease: Mika Kivimäki, Jane E. Ferrie, Eric Brunner, Jenny Head, Martin J. Shipley, Jussi Vahtera, and Michael G. Marmot, "Justice at Work and Reduced Risk of Coronary Heart Disease Among Employees: The Whitehall II Study," *Archives of Internal Medicine* 165, no. 19 (2005): 2245–2251.

12   *deal with possible assholes:* Robert I. Sutton, *The No Asshole Rule: Building a Civilized Workplace and Surviving One That Isn't* (New York: Business Plus, 2010, paperback edition), 197.

national surveys: 2014 WBI U.S. Workplace Bullying Survey, accessed October 26, 2016, http://www.workplacebullying .org/wbiresearch/wbi-2014-us-survey/; 2007 WBI U.S. Workplace Bullying Survey, accessed October 26, 2016, http://www .workplacebullying.org/multi/pdf/WBIsurvey2007.pdf.

2. ASSHOLE ASSESSMENT: HOW BAD IS THE PROBLEM?

15   *"targeted a false accusation at you":* Kathryne E. Dupré, Julian Barling, and Kimberly-Anne Dawe, "Harm to Those Who Serve: Effects of Direct and Vicarious Customer-Initiated Workplace Aggression," *Journal of Interpersonal Violence* 29, no. 13 (2014): 2355–2377, 2364.

Abusive Supervision Scale: Bennett J. Tepper, "Consequences of Abusive Supervision," *Academy of Management Journal* 43, no. 2 (2000): 178–190.

16 *"The Rude Stranger in Everyday Life"*: Philip R. Smith, Timothy L. Phillips, and Ryan D. King, *Incivility: The Rude Stranger in Everyday Life* (Cambridge, MA: Cambridge University Press, 2010), 25, 27.

"cognitive minefield": Daniel Kahneman, *Thinking, Fast and Slow* (New York: Macmillan, 2011), 417.

"Don't just do something, stand there": Jerome E. Groopman, *How Doctors Think* (Boston: Houghton Mifflin, 2007), 169.

23 *"hardened to other people in general"*: Smith, Phillips, and King, *Incivility*, 119.

24 *abusive supervision:* Jeremy D. Mackey, Rachel E. Frieder, Jeremy R. Brees, and Mark J. Martinko, "Abusive Supervision: A Meta-Analysis and Empirical Review," *Journal of Management* (2015), doi: 10.1177/0149206315573997.

bullied schoolchildren: See, for example, Amy L. Gower and Iris W. Borowsky, "Associations Between Frequency of Bullying Involvement and Adjustment in Adolescence," *Academic Pediatrics* 13, no. 3 (2013): 214–221.

"worse about themselves": Robert I. Sutton, *The No Asshole Rule: Building a Civilized Workplace and Surviving One That Isn't* (New York: Business Plus, 2007), 11.

25 *selfish and greedy they become:* Yoram Bauman and Elaina Rose, "Selection or Indoctrination: Why Do Economics Students Donate Less Than the Rest?" *Journal of Economic Behavior & Organization* 79, no. 3 (2011): 318–327.

strategic nastiness: Barry M. Staw, Katherine A. DeCelles, and Peter Degoey, "Leadership in the Locker Room: The Effect of Coaches' Unpleasant Emotion at Halftime on Subsequent Team Performance" (unpublished manuscript, University of California at Berkeley, 2015).

28 *"opposites attract"*: Robert B. Cialdini, *Influence: The Psychology of Persuasion*, rev. ed. (New York: Harper Business, 2006).

"The Waiter Spit in My Soup!": Emily M. Hunter and Lisa M. Penney, "The Waiter Spit in My Soup! Antecedents of Customer-Directed Counterproductive Work Behavior," *Human Performance* 27, no. 3 (2014): 262–281.

29   *just jerks pretending to be organizations:* Barry M. Staw, "Dressing Up Like an Organization: When Psychological Theories Can Explain Organizational Action," *Journal of Management* 17, no. 4 (1991): 805–819.

31   *"persecute and inflict misery":* Carlos Castaneda, *The Fire from Within* (New York: Simon & Schuster, 1984), 17.

32   *"don't have admiration or respect for it":* Nathanael J. Fast, Nir Halevy, and Adam D. Galinsky, "The Destructive Nature of Power Without Status," *Journal of Experimental Social Psychology* 48, no. 1 (2012): 391–394.

35   Give and Take: Adam Grant, *Give and Take: Why Helping Others Drives Our Success* (New York: Penguin, 2013).

3. MAKE A CLEAN GETAWAY

38   *spat at, tailgated:* Philip R. Smith, Timothy L. Phillips, and Ryan D. King, *Incivility: The Rude Stranger in Everyday Life* (Cambridge, MA: Cambridge University Press, 2010) 25.

more abuse in the future: Dana Yagil, "When the Customer Is Wrong: A Review of Research on Aggression and Sexual Harassment in Service Encounters," *Aggression and Violent Behavior* 13, no. 2 (2008): 141–152.

quit their jobs: Bennett J. Tepper, "Consequences of Abusive Supervision," *Academy of Management Journal* 43, no. 2 (2000): 178–190.

take their business elsewhere: Christine Porath, Debbie MacInnis, and Valerie Folkes, "Witnessing Incivility Among Employees: Effects on Consumer Anger and Negative Inferences About Companies," *Journal of Consumer Research* 37, no. 2 (2010): 292–303.

41 *"our lives sunk into it":* Robert I. Sutton, *The No Asshole Rule: Building a Civilized Workplace and Surviving One That Isn't* (New York: Business Plus, 2007), 98.

46 *negative reactions in their supervisors:* Anthony C. Klotz and Mark C. Bolino, "Saying Goodbye: The Nature, Causes, and Consequences of Employee Resignation Styles," *Journal of Applied Psychology* 101, no. 10 (2016): 1386.

49 *"people leave bosses, not companies":* Robert I. Sutton, *Good Boss, Bad Boss: How to Be the Best . . . and Learn from the Worst* (New York: Business Plus, 2010).

50 *more prestigious and dignified work:* Nathalie Louit-Martinod, Cécile Chanut-Guieu, Cathel Kornig, and Philippe Méhaut, "'A plus Dans le Bus': Work-Related Stress Among French Bus Drivers," *SAGE Open* 6, no. 1 (2016), doi: 10.1177/2158244016629393.

53 *debates via text messages:* Noam Lapidot-Lefler and Azy Barak, "Effects of Anonymity, Invisibility, and Lack of Eye-Contact on Toxic Online Disinhibition," *Computers in Human Behavior* 28, no. 2 (2012): 434–443.

65 "and how you do it": Quote from Sutton, *Good Boss, Bad Boss*, 183.

4. ASSHOLE AVOIDANCE TECHNIQUES: REDUCING YOUR EXPOSURE

68 *treat others like dirt:* M. Sandy Hershcovis and Tara C. Reich, "Integrating Workplace Aggression Research: Relational, Contextual, and Method Considerations," *Journal of Organizational Behavior* 34, no. S1 (2013): S26–S42.

"stress contagion": Eva Oberle and Kimberly A. Schonert-Reichl, "Stress Contagion in the Classroom? The Link Between Classroom Teacher Burnout and Morning Cortisol in Elementary School Students," *Social Science & Medicine* 159 (2016): 30–37.

"like the common cold": Trevor Foulk, Andrew Woolum, and

Amir Erez, "Catching Rudeness Is Like Catching a Cold: The Contagion Effects of Low-Intensity Negative Behaviors," *Journal of Applied Psychology* 101, no. 1 (2016): 50.

69 *closer people sat to one another:* Thomas J. Allen, *Managing the Flow of Technology: Technology Transfer and the Dissemination of Technological Information Within the R&D Organization* (Cambridge, MA: MIT Press Books, 1984).

via email, texts, and social media: David Krackhardt, "Constraints on the Interactive Organization as an Ideal Type," *Networks in the Knowledge Economy* (Oxford: Oxford University Press, 2003), 324–335; Ben Waber, Jennifer Magnolfi, and Greg Lindsay, "Workspaces That Move People," *Harvard Business Review* 92, no. 10 (2014): 68–77.

71 *workplace bullies:* Pamela Lutgen-Sandvik, "Take This Job and . . . : Quitting and Other Forms of Resistance to Workplace Bullying," *Communication Monographs* 73, no. 4 (2006): 406–433.

72 *"too busy to go to the office":* Lutgen-Sandvik, "Take This Job and . . . ," 419.

73 *"aggressive conduct disorder":* Jean Decety, Kalina J. Michalska, Yuko Akitsuki, and Benjamin B. Lahey, "Atypical Empathic Responses in Adolescents with Aggressive Conduct Disorder: A Functional MRI Investigation," *Biological Psychology* 80, no. 2 (2009): 203–211.

75 *interviewing the real collectors:* Robert I. Sutton, "Maintaining Norms About Expressed Emotions: The Case of Bill Collectors," *Administrative Science Quarterly* 36, no. 2 (1991): 245–268.

"they start to tone it down": Sutton, "Maintaining Norms," 262.

77 *distressing and boring work:* Curtis K. Chan and Michel Anteby, "Task Segregation as a Mechanism for Within-Job Inequality: Women and Men of the Transportation Security Administration," *Administrative Science Quarterly* 61, no. 2 (2016): 184–216; Michel Anteby and Curtis K. Chan, "Being Seen *and* Going Un-

noticed" (unpublished manuscript, Harvard Business School, 2012).

78 *"interchangeable mass of travelers"*: Anteby and Chan, "Being Seen," 29.

"deal with them at all": Chan and Anteby, "Task Segregation," 198.

81 *"his or her charges"*: Robert I. Sutton, *Good Boss, Bad Boss: How to Be the Best . . . and Learn from the Worst* (New York: Business Plus, 2010), 154.

82 *flak catchers are "lightning rods"*: Paul G. Friedman, "Hassle Handling: Front-Line Diplomacy in the Work-Place," *Business Communication Quarterly* 47, no. 1 (1984): 30–33.

"jolts sent by the dissatisfied": Friedman, "Hassle Handling," 30.

83 *spares dentists*: Alma M. Rodríguez⊠Sánchez, Jari J. Hakanen, Riku Perhoniemi, and Marisa Salanova, "With a Little Help from My Assistant: Buffering the Negative Effects of Emotional Dissonance on Dentist Performance," *Community Dentistry and Oral Epidemiology* 41, no. 5 (2013): 415–423.

85 *or onstage, performances*: Erving Goffman, *The Presentation of Self in Everyday Life* (Harmondsworth: Penguin, 1978).

pinch her behind: Robert I. Sutton, *The No Asshole Rule: Building a Civilized Workplace and Surviving One That Isn't* (New York: Business Plus, 2007), 21–22.

88 *bathrooms as backstage areas*: Spencer E. Cahill, William Distler, Cynthia Lachowetz, Andrea Meaney, Robyn Tarallo, and Teena Willard, "Meanwhile Backstage: Public Bathrooms and the Interaction Order," *Journal of Contemporary Ethnography* 14, no. 1 (1985): 33–58.

"demands of public life": Cahill, Distler, Lachowetz, Meaney, Tarallo, and Willard, "Meanwhile Backstage," 37.

"wept for several minutes": Cahill, Distler, Lachowetz, Meaney, Tarallo, and Willard, "Meanwhile Backstage," 50.

5. MIND TRICKS THAT PROTECT YOUR SOUL

97   *more constructive behaviors:* Judith S. Beck, *Cognitive Behavior Therapy: Basics and Beyond* (New York: Guilford Press, 2011).

research on such reframing: Adam L. Alter, Joshua Aronson, John M. Darley, Cordaro Rodriguez, and Diane N. Ruble, "Rising to the Threat: Reducing Stereotype Threat by Reframing the Threat as a Challenge," *Journal of Experimental Social Psychology* 46, no. 1 (2010): 166–171.

98   *emotional shelter:* Dana Yagil, Hasida Ben-Zur, and Inbal Tamir, "Do Employees Cope Effectively with Abusive Supervision at Work? An Exploratory Study," *International Journal of Stress Management* 18, no. 1 (2011): 5.

nasty rumors about them: Bernardo Moreno-Jiménez, Alfredo Rodríguez-Muñoz, Juan Carlos Pastor, Ana Isabel Sanz-Vergel, and Eva Garrosa, "The Moderating Effects of Psychological Detachment and Thoughts of Revenge in Workplace Bullying," *Personality and Individual Differences* 46, no. 3 (2009): 359–364.

100   *"interpretations for their behavior":* Beck, *Cognitive Behavior Therapy,* 182.

101   *pictures of angry people:* Jens Blechert, Gal Sheppes, Carolina Di Tella, Hants Williams, and James J. Gross, "See What You Think: Reappraisal Modulates Behavioral and Neural Responses to Social Stimuli," *Psychological Science* 23, no. 4 (2012): 346–353.

in U.S. state prisons: Katherine DeCelles and Michel Anteby, "Caring in the Clink: How Agents of Total Institutions Show Empathy for Captives" (unpublished manuscript, University of Toronto, 2016).

blamed for their plight: DeCelles and Anteby, "Caring in the Clink," 32–34.

102   *"time wounds all heels":* Robert I. Sutton, *The No Asshole Rule:*

Building a Civilized Workplace and Surviving One That Isn't (New York: Business Plus, 2007), 26.

"less disastrous conclusion": Beck, *Cognitive Behavior Therapy*, 181.

109 *Unforgiving thoughts had the opposite effects:* Charlotte van Oyen Witvliet, Thomas E. Ludwig, and Kelly L. Vander Laan, "Granting Forgiveness or Harboring Grudges: Implications for Emotion, Physiology, and Health," *Psychological Science* 12, no. 2 (2001): 117–123.

research on bullied schoolchildren: Luke A. Egan and Natasha Todorov, "Forgiveness as a Coping Strategy to Allow School Students to Deal with the Effects of Being Bullied: Theoretical and Empirical Discussion," *Journal of Social and Clinical Psychology* 28, no. 2 (2009): 198.

coated in humor or sarcasm: Rod A. Martin, *The Psychology of Humor: An Integrative Approach* (Cambridge, MA: Academic Press, 2010).

"Coping Humor Scale": Rod A. Martin and Herbert M. Lefcourt, "Sense of Humor as a Moderator of the Relation Between Stressors and Moods," *Journal of Personality and Social Psychology* 45, no. 6 (1983): 1313.

"even in trying situations": Martin and Lefcourt, "Sense of Humor," 1316.

110 *serve as protective armor:* Annie Hogh and Andrea Dofradottir, "Coping with Bullying in the Workplace," *European Journal of Work and Organizational Psychology* 10, no. 4 (2001): 485–495.

111 *"imagining the future"*: Emma Bruehlman-Senecal and Ozlem Ayduk, "This Too Shall Pass: Temporal Distance and the Regulation of Emotional Distress," *Journal of Personality and Social Psychology* 108, no. 2 (2015): 356.

"problem will fade over time": Bruehlman-Senecal and Ayduk, "This Too Shall Pass," 361.

112 *plagues many organizations and teams:* See, for example, James K. Harter, Frank L. Schmidt, and Corey L. M. Keyes, "Well-Being in the Workplace and Its Relationship to Business Outcomes: A Review of the Gallup Studies," *Flourishing: Positive Psychology and the Life Well-Lived* 2 (2003): 205–224.

infections among patients: Jeannie P. Cimiotti, Linda H. Aiken, Douglas M. Sloane, and Evan S. Wu, "Nurse Staffing, Burnout, and Health Care–Associated Infection," *American Journal of Infection Control* 40, no. 6 (2012): 486–490.

113 *to use this mind trick:* Sutton, *No Asshole Rule,* 134–136.

114 *conflict between work and family roles:* Sabine Sonnentag and Charlotte Fritz, "Recovery from Job Stress: The Stressor⊠Detachment Model as an Integrative Framework," *Journal of Organizational Behavior* 36, no. S1 (2015): S72–S103.

115 *physically "dirty":* Katherine DeCelles and Chen-Bo Zhong, "Beyond the Bars: Impurities of Prison Work and Implications for Worker Well-Being and Work-Home Conflict" (unpublished manuscript, University of Toronto, 2016).

"'not take it home'": DeCelles and Zhong, "Beyond the Bars," 21–22.

116 *disdain and disrespect:* Gillian Dolan, Esben Strodl, and Elisabeth Hamernik, "Why Renal Nurses Cope So Well with Their Workplace Stressors," *Journal of Renal Care* 38, no. 4 (2012): 222–232.

"do what I have to do": Dolan, Strodl, and Hamernik, "Why Renal Nurses Cope," 228.

"fake positive emotions": Ashley E. Nixon, Valentina Bruk⊠Lee, and Paul E. Spector, "Grin and Bear It?: Employees' Use of Surface Acting During Co⊠worker Conflict," *Stress and Health* (2016): 9.

118 *"feels like a prolonged personal insult":* Sutton, *No Asshole Rule,* 135.

119 *and are less productive:* Numerous studies on the costs of disen-

gagement are summarized at www.gallup.com. See, for example, Marco Nink, "The Negative Impact of Disengaged Employees on Germany," April 5, 2016, accessed October 29, 2016, http://www.gallup.com/businessjournal/190445/negative-impact-disengaged-employees-germany.aspx.

6. FIGHTING BACK

123 *springing into action:* Daniel Kahneman, *Thinking, Fast and Slow* (New York: Macmillan, 2011), 417.

125 *New York, Colorado, and Virginia:* See "Tape-Recording Laws at a Glance," Reporters Committee, accessed October 29, 2016, http://www.rcfp.org/reporters-recording-guide/tape-recording-laws-glance.

126 *in the most innocent actions:* MeowLan Evelyn Chan and Daniel J. McAllister, "Abusive Supervision Through the Lens of Employee State Paranoia," *Academy of Management Review* 39, no. 1 (2014): 44–66.

127 *intercepted his mail:* Roderick M. Kramer and Dana A. Gavrieli, "Power, Uncertainty, and the Amplification of Doubt: An Archival Study of Suspicion Inside the Oval Office," *Trust and Distrust in Organizations: Dilemmas and Approaches* (New York: Russell Sage Foundation, 2004), 342–370.
   employees were fired: Pamela Lutgen-Sandvik, "Take This Job and . . . : Quitting and Other Forms of Resistance to Workplace Bullying," *Communication Monographs* 73, no. 4 (2006): 424.

128 *so scared anymore:* Lutgen-Sandvik, "Take This Job and . . . ," 416.

130 *"righteous anger":* Dirk Lindebaum and Deanna Geddes, "The Place and Role of (Moral) Anger in Organizational Behavior Studies," *Journal of Organizational Behavior* 37 (2016): 738–757.

131 *"but here it is now":* Mary Soames, *Winston and Clementine: The Personal Letters of the Churchills* (New York: Houghton Mifflin Harcourt, 2001), 486.

Never Call Them Jerks: Arthur Paul Boers, *Never Call Them Jerks* (Rowman & Littlefield, 1999).

132   *Machiavellian personalities:* Christian Jarrett, "The Neuroscience of Being a Selfish Jerk," *Science of Us,* accessed October 29, 2016, http://nymag.com/scienceofus/2015/08/neuroscience -of-being-a-selfish-jerk.html.

"porcupine power": Roderick M. Kramer, "The Great Intimidators," *Harvard Business Review* 84, no. 2 (2006): 88.

137   *who question their judgment:* Michael Maccoby, "Narcissistic Leaders: The Incredible Pros, the Inevitable Cons," *Harvard Business Review* 78, no. 1 (2000): 68–78.

"a group of yes-men": Maccoby, "Narcissistic Leaders," 73.

139   *"traded in the Bible":* Eric Jaffe, "The Complicated Psychology of Revenge," *Observer* 24, no. 8 (2011), accessed October 29, 2016, http://www.psychologicalscience.org/publications/observer /2011/october-11/the-complicated-psychology-of-revenge.html.

"'he was not happy'": Robert I. Sutton, *The No Asshole Rule: Building a Civilized Workplace and Surviving One That Isn't* (New York: Business Plus, 2007), 147–148.

findings from a study: Harvey A. Hornstein, "Boss Abuse and Subordinate Payback," *Journal of Applied Behavioral Science* 52, no. 2 (2016): 231–239.

"Successful payback": Hornstein, "Boss Abuse," 236.

140   *"she wasn't kidding":* Sutton, *No Asshole Rule,* 188–189.

141   *didn't stop the abuse:* Hornstein, "Boss Abuse," 237.

lion's share of the prize money: Kevin M. Carlsmith, Timothy D. Wilson, and Daniel T. Gilbert, "The Paradoxical Consequences of Revenge," *Journal of Personality and Social Psychology* 95, no. 6 (2008): 1316.

142   *"focus on something different":* Jaffe, "Psychology of Revenge."

"heal, and do well": Carlsmith, Wilson, and Gilbert, "Paradoxical Consequences of Revenge," 1324.

impulse to "get even": Thomas M. Tripp and Robert J. Bies, *Getting Even: The Truth About Workplace Revenge — and How to Stop It* (San Francisco: John Wiley & Sons, 2009).

"the other's unwarranted actions": Robert J. Bies, Thomas M. Tripp, and Roderick M. Kramer, "At the Breaking Point: Cognitive and Social Dynamics of Revenge in Organizations," in Robert A. Giacalone and Jerald Greenberg, eds., *Antisocial Behavior in Organizations* (Thousand Oaks, CA: Sage, 1997), 23.

144 *"I own the place and it owns me"*: Robert I. Sutton and Huggy Rao, *Scaling Up Excellence: Getting to More Without Settling for Less* (New York: Crown Business, 2014), 144.

145 *harder to stop than good behaviors:* Roy F. Baumeister, Ellen Bratslavsky, Catrin Finkenauer, and Kathleen D. Vohs, "Bad Is Stronger Than Good," *Review of General Psychology* 5, no. 4 (2001): 323.

"bad apples": Will Felps, Terence R. Mitchell, and Eliza Byington, "How, When, and Why Bad Apples Spoil the Barrel: Negative Group Members and Dysfunctional Groups," *Research in Organizational Behavior* 27 (2006): 175–222.

146 *doesn't fire them right away:* Laszlo Bock, *Work Rules!: Insights from Inside Google That Will Transform How You Live and Lead* (New York: Twelve, 2015).

147 *"big personalities"*: Sutton and Rao, *Scaling Up Excellence,* 235–237.
enjoy spending time together: Robert B. Cialdini, *Influence: The Psychology of Persuasion,* rev. ed. (New York, Harper Business, 2006).

149 *adopted in fifty U.S. states:* See "Policies & Laws," Stopbullying.gov, accessed October 30, 2016, https://www.stopbullying.gov/laws/.

150 *weak and ineffective:* Jaana Juvonen and Sandra Graham, "Bullying in Schools: The Power of Bullies and the Plight of Victims," *Annual Review of Psychology* 65 (2014): 159–185.

156 *"upward hostility" to supervisors:* Bennett J. Tepper, Marie S.

Mitchell, Dana L. Haggard, Ho Kwong Kwan, and Hee☒man Park, "On the Exchange of Hostility with Supervisors: An Examination of Self☒Enhancing and Self☒Defeating Perspectives," *Personnel Psychology* 68, no. 4 (2015): 723–758.

7. BE PART OF THE SOLUTION, NOT THE PROBLEM

159 *"browbeaters, bullies, and bastards":* Robert I. Sutton, *The No Asshole Rule: Building a Civilized Workplace and Surviving One That Isn't* (New York: Business Plus, 2007), 97–99.

160 *"Ochsner 10/5 Way":* Christine Porath, *Mastering Civility: A Manifesto for the Workplace* (New York: Grand Central, 2016), 46.

163 You Are Now Less Dumb: David McRaney, *You Are Now Less Dumb* (New York: Penguin, 2013).
"friendship continued to his death": McRaney, *Now Less Dumb,* 59.

164 *"love those you help":* McRaney, *Now Less Dumb,* 70.

165 *exaggerate them in their own minds:* Justin Kruger and David Dunning, "Unskilled and Unaware of It: How Difficulties in Recognizing One's Own Incompetence Lead to Inflated Self-Assessments," *Journal of Personality and Social Psychology* 77, no. 6 (1999): 1121; Oliver J. Sheldon, David Dunning, and Daniel R. Ames, "Emotionally Unskilled, Unaware, and Uninterested in Learning More: Reactions to Feedback About Deficits in Emotional Intelligence," *Journal of Applied Psychology* 99, no. 1 (2014): 125.

166 *the worst person to ask:* Heidi Grant Halvorson, *No One Understands You and What to Do About It* (Boston: Harvard Business Review Press, 2015), 121–125.

167 *"kind as you used to be":* Mary Soames, *Winston and Clementine: The Personal Letters of the Churchills* (New York: Houghton Mifflin Harcourt, 2001), 486.

168 *once had little power:* Melissa J. Williams, Deborah H. Gruenfeld, and Lucia E. Guillory, "Sexual Aggression When Power Is

New: Effects of Acute High Power on Chronically Low-Power Individuals," *Journal of Personality and Social Psychology* (2016), in press.

star underlings: Sherry Moss, "Why Some Bosses Bully Their Best Employees," June 7, 2016, *Harvard Business Review,* accessed November 1, 2016, https://hbr.org/2016/06/why-some-bosses-bully-their-best-employees.

169 *"cold" person:* Selma Carolin Rudert, Leonie Reutner, Rainer Greifeneder, and Mirella Walker, "Faced with Exclusion: Perceived Facial Warmth and Competence Influence Moral Judgments of Social Exclusion," *Journal of Experimental Social Psychology* 68 (2017): 101–112.

your martyrdom: Heidi Grant Halvorson, "Signs You Might Be a Toxic Colleague," March 2, 2016, *Harvard Business Review,* accessed November 1, 2016, https://hbr.org/2016/03/signs-you-might-be-a-toxic-colleague.

"Rule Nazi": Halvorson, "Toxic Colleague."

enough sleep: Christopher J. Budnick and Larissa K. Barber, "Behind Sleepy Eyes: Implications of Sleep Loss for Organizations and Employees," *Translational Issues in Psychological Science* 1, no. 1 (2015): 89.

a woman for a boss: Ekaterina Netchaeva, Maryam Kouchaki, and Leah D. Sheppard, "A Man's (Precarious) Place: Men's Experienced Threat and Self-Assertive Reactions to Female Superiors," *Personality and Social Psychology Bulletin* 41, no. 9 (2015): 1247–1259.

(some people are like that): Justin Hepler and Dolores Albarracín, "Attitudes Without Objects: Evidence for a Dispositional Attitude, Its Measurement, and Its Consequences," *Journal of Personality and Social Psychology* 104, no. 6 (2013): 1060.

prone to become "carriers": Trevor Foulk, Andrew Woolum, and Amir Erez, "Catching Rudeness Is Like Catching a Cold: The

Contagion Effects of Low-Intensity Negative Behaviors," *Journal of Applied Psychology* 101, no. 1 (2016): 51.

171 *50% of the time:* Dacher Keltner, *The Power Paradox: How We Gain and Lose Influence* (New York: Penguin, 2016), 121–125.

174 *decisions did not suffer:* Allen C. Bluedorn, Daniel B. Turban, and Mary Sue Love, "The Effects of Stand-up and Sit-down Meeting Formats on Meeting Outcomes," *Journal of Applied Psychology* 84, no. 2 (1999): 277.

177 *element of a good and effective apology:* Roy J. Lewicki, Beth Polin, and Robert B. Lount, "An Exploration of the Structure of Effective Apologies," *Negotiation and Conflict Management Research* 9, no. 2 (2016): 177–196.

179 *after his or her emotional storms:* Peter J. Frost, *Toxic Emotions at Work* (Boston: Harvard Business School Press, 2003), 75–77.

181 *"mental time travel":* Emma Bruehlman-Senecal and Ozlem Ayduk, "This Too Shall Pass: Temporal Distance and the Regulation of Emotional Distress," *Journal of Personality and Social Psychology* 108, no. 2 (2015): 356.
    look back from the future: See research and writings on premortems including Gary Klein, "Performing a Project Premortem," *Harvard Business Review* 85, no. 9 (2007): 18–19; Robert I. Sutton and Huggy Rao, *Scaling Up Excellence: Getting to More Without Settling for Less* (New York: Crown Business, 2014), 264–270.

183 *"decency and good manners":* Edward O. Wilson, *Sociobiology* (Boston: Harvard University Press, 2000), 257.

Index

CPSIA information can be obtained
at www.ICGtesting.com
Printed in the USA
LVHW091432131218
600011LV00027B/156/P

9 781328 511669